PROCRASTINATION FOR OVERACHIEVERS

A Humorous Guide to Doing Absolutely Nothing Efficiently

AVERY WELLS

Contents

Introduction

Let's face it: procrastination gets a bad rap. It's the lazy villain of motivational speeches, the sinister foil to productivity gurus, and the shadowy nemesis of to-do lists everywhere. But what if I told you that procrastination—yes, that thing you're probably doing right now instead of something important—isn't all bad? What if, instead of a failure, procrastination is just an unexpected detour on the scenic route to getting things done?

Think about it: some of your best ideas might have popped up while you were doing anything but the task at hand. Whether it's a last-minute flash of brilliance the night before a deadline or a genius insight that hits you in the shower after hours of avoiding work, procrastination has a funny way of delivering. It's not just avoidance—it's incubation. Letting your brain marinate in chaos can sometimes yield surprising clarity. See? You're not a slacker; you're a visionary in disguise.

It's time to stop beating yourself up about procrastination and start recognizing its potential. Let's reframe it: procrastination isn't the enemy; it's a misunderstood sidekick. Sure, it might delay things a bit, but it's also your subconscious whispering, "Hey, maybe this isn't the time—or maybe we need a snack first." This book isn't about overcoming procrastination but learning to wield it like a superpower.

By embracing the art of doing nothing efficiently, you'll discover that procrastination isn't just a roadblock—it's a shortcut. You'll learn how to make progress even when it feels like you're just spinning your wheels, turning downtime into prime time. With a little guidance, procrastination can go from being your Achilles' heel to your secret weapon.

If procrastination were an Olympic sport, you'd have a gold medal and a sponsorship deal by now. The cycle is all too familiar: you start with the best intentions, armed with planners, sticky notes, and color-coded spreadsheets. You're ready to conquer the world—or at least your inbox. Then, five hours later, you're deep-diving into YouTube tutorials on how to fold fitted sheets, wondering where the day went.

The truth is procrastinators are secretly master strategists. Who else can stretch a 20-minute task into an all-day extravaganza, complete with snacks, existential crises, and a fully reorganized closet? It's not inefficiency; it's performance art.

This book isn't about guilt-tripping you into productivity. You've already got enough voices in your head doing that (hi, inner critic). Instead, it's about showing you how to work with your natural tendencies rather than fighting against them. You'll learn how to embrace the ebb and flow of motivation, use procrastination to fuel your creativity, and—dare I say it—actually get things done without sacrificing your sanity.

So, grab a cup of coffee (or whatever you use to fuel your avoidance tactics), settle into your favorite procrastination nook, and get ready to redefine what it means to be "productive." By the end of this book, you'll have mastered the fine art of procrastinating like a pro—efficiently, effectively, and without an ounce of guilt. Now, doesn't that sound like something worth putting off everything else for?

ONE

Understanding Your Procrastination Style

Procrastination comes in many forms. Some people procrastinate with finesse, others with flair, and a few of us turn it into an Olympic sport. You might think procrastination is just avoiding work, but oh no—it's a much more nuanced art form. Maybe you're the meticulous Over-Planner, armed with a highlighter and enough sticky notes to wallpaper a mansion. Or perhaps you're the dreamy Daydreamer, coming up with revolutionary ideas that you'll totally start on... tomorrow. And let's not forget the Busy-Work Procrastinator, the master of looking productive while actually doing nothing of consequence.

The truth is, procrastination isn't just one-size-fits-all. It's a buffet of habits and coping mechanisms, each with its quirks and, dare I say, hidden strengths. This chapter is all about understanding your procrastination style—because the first step to mastering the art of doing nothing efficiently is figuring out *how* you do nothing in the first place. Spoiler: once you know your style, you can use it to your advantage.

Whether you're color-coding a to-do list you have no intention of completing, getting lost in a three-hour Pinterest rabbit hole labeled "research," or alphabetizing your sock drawer when a deadline looms, there's a method to your madness. And guess what? With the right tweaks, you can turn your procrastination into productivity. Well, *almost* productivity—but let's not get carried away.

So, let's dive in, laugh at our own quirks, and figure out how to turn our unique procrastination tendencies into something vaguely useful. After all, if you're going to procrastinate, you might as well do it with style.

The Over-Planner: Procrastinating by "Organizing" and "Researching"

You sit down to start your project, coffee steaming gently beside you, a fresh notebook in front of you, and a perfectly sharpened pencil at the ready. "This is it," you tell yourself. "Today is the day I'm going to crush this task." But wait—how can you possibly get started without creating a detailed timeline first? And shouldn't you outline every step? And maybe color-code your priorities while you're at it? Suddenly, hours have gone by, and you've accomplished... absolutely nothing. But your to-do list? It's a work of art.

Welcome to the world of the Over-Planner: a procrastination style so sneaky it convinces you that you're being productive when you're actually just avoiding the real work. Over-Planners excel at preparing to work, but the actual "doing" part? That's where things get tricky. Why dive into the messy, unpredictable task when you could spend another two hours perfecting the plan for tackling it?

The appeal of over-planning is that it feels safe. When you're organizing, outlining, and researching, there's no risk of failure, no chance of mistakes, and no need to confront the scary reality of starting. It's like procrastination's polished cousin, the one that wears a blazer and carries a clipboard to make you think they're legitimate. Over-planning makes you feel busy, even though your tasks are more about shuffling papers than moving mountains.

Let's not pretend it's all bad, though. Over-Planners do have some valuable skills. You're detail-oriented, thorough, and probably great at anticipating potential roadblocks. But when planning becomes an endless loop, it's time to call it what it is: glorified stalling. That 14-tab spreadsheet you made to track your progress? Impressive, yes. Necessary? Probably not.

So, how do you break free from the Over-Planner trap? The first step is recognizing when your planning has crossed the line from preparation to procrastination. Here's a hint: if you've spent more time "researching" how to do a task than it would take to actually *do* the task, you're probably over-planning. Reading one or two articles to get started? Smart. Diving into a three-hour deep dive on historical paperclip designs because you're writing a report about office efficiency? Not so much.

The next step is to set boundaries for your planning time. If you're working on a project, give yourself a specific amount of time to outline, research, or organize before diving in. For example, spend 30 minutes mapping out the key points of your essay, then start writing —even if your outline isn't perfect. This approach forces you to move from planning to doing without getting stuck in the weeds.

Another strategy is to embrace the concept of the "minimum viable plan." Instead of creating an elaborate, step-by-step roadmap, focus on the bare essentials you need to get started. Think of it like plotting a road trip: you don't need to know every gas station you'll stop at, just the general route and maybe a playlist. Once you're on the road, you can adjust as you go.

If your inner Over-Planner balks at the idea of jumping in without a fully fleshed-out plan, remind yourself that *done is better than perfect*. A half-baked draft is still more useful than the most detailed outline in the world if that outline never makes it off the page. Progress, not perfection, should be your mantra.

Over-Planners can also benefit from external accountability. Share your timeline with a friend or coworker and ask them to check in on your progress. Knowing someone else is watching can help curb your tendency to tweak and refine endlessly.

And finally, learn to laugh at your over-planning tendencies. When you catch yourself organizing your pens by ink flow instead of tackling your big project, don't beat yourself up—smile and acknowledge the ridiculousness of it. Awareness is half the battle, and a little humor goes a long way.

The Over-Planner procrastination style may be sneaky, but it's not invincible. With a little self-awareness, some time limits, and a commitment to action, you can channel your love of preparation into actual progress. Just remember: at some point, you have to put down the sticky notes and pick up the work. Your beautifully color-coded plan will thank you later.

The Daydreamer: Creative Distractions That Lead to Ideas, Not Action

You sit down to work. The laptop hums, the coffee steams, and the task is clear. But then—wait! What if you finally designed that dream treehouse? Or started your memoir, "Confessions of a Procrastinating Genius"? Before you know it, an hour has passed, and you've mentally launched three businesses, planned a trip to Iceland, and imagined your future career as a goat whisperer. Welcome to the Daydreamer's world, where creative distractions rule and productivity politely waits in the corner.

Daydreaming is, quite frankly, a fantastic way to procrastinate. While everyone else is stressing about deadlines, you're imagining a better world—one where coffee refills itself, socks never get lost, and you're being interviewed about your groundbreaking invention that turns leftovers into gourmet meals. It's fun, it's exciting, and let's face it, it's way better than spreadsheets. The only downside? Those brilliant ideas rarely translate into actual accomplishments.

The Daydreamer procrastination style thrives on imagination. Your brain doesn't just wander; it takes a first-class trip to fantasyland. While this is delightful for creativity, it's not exactly helpful when there's an overdue report or a mountain of laundry begging for your attention. Still, let's not sell your wandering mind short—daydreaming is a superpower when used correctly.

First, let's address why daydreaming feels so appealing. It's easy. There's no risk of failure in your imagination. The app you designed in your head works flawlessly, your book is a bestseller, and no one in Fantasyland points out that you haven't actually started anything. It's the ultimate escape, free from the pesky realities of hard work, rejection, or, heaven forbid, feedback.

But science says you're onto something. Studies show that daydreaming can boost creativity and problem-solving skills. Your brain is connecting dots in the background, even when it seems like you're doing nothing. That flash of brilliance during your morning shower or the inspired solution while folding socks? That's daydreaming working its subtle magic. The trick is turning those dreams into action.

To harness your daydreaming superpowers, start by writing things down. Keep a notebook, app, or even a sticky note handy for capturing those ideas. No matter how wild, silly, or impractical, jot them down. This habit turns your wandering thoughts into a treasure chest of possibilities instead of a fleeting cloud of "I had a great idea, but I forgot what it was."

Next, set boundaries for your flights of fancy. Schedule specific "daydream breaks" where you let your mind wander freely—like letting a puppy off the leash at a park. These breaks could be 10–15 minutes between work sessions or during a relaxing walk. Once the timer goes off, it's time to refocus. By structuring your creative escapades, you prevent them from hijacking your entire day.

If you're in the middle of a work session and catch yourself drifting into daydream territory, try redirecting that energy toward your task. Stuck on a presentation? Imagine delivering it to a packed audience, complete with a standing ovation. Can't figure out how to start your project? Pretend you're pitching it to your hero. Channeling your imagination into what you need to do can make it feel less like work and more like a creative challenge.

And here's the real kicker: act on one of your ideas. Just one. No, you don't have to launch the goat-whispering business tomorrow, but you could sketch a logo or look up what goats eat (spoiler: everything). Taking a single small step toward a daydream brings it out of fantasyland and into reality. Plus, it feels incredibly satisfying to make progress on something you once only imagined.

Daydreamers, your mind is a playground, and that's a gift. But don't let your playground stay empty. Choose one swing set, climb aboard, and give it a push. Dream big, but don't forget to act small. Because while castles in the sky are lovely, the real magic happens when you start building them on the ground.

The Busy-Work Procrastinator: Doing Low-Priority Tasks to Avoid Big Ones

You know you're a Busy-Work Procrastinator when your day is packed with activity, but your actual goals? Still sitting there, untouched, wondering when you'll get around to them. Sure, you've reorganized the sock drawer (again), answered emails that didn't need answering, and spent an hour creating folders for "2025 Tax Prep," even though it's November. You're *busy*—but not where it counts.

The Busy-Work Procrastinator excels at appearing productive. You're vacuuming the corners of your office when that big project is due, fine-tuning a spreadsheet that no one but you will ever see, or rearranging the bookshelf by genre and then by vibe. And the best part? It all feels justified. *"A clean desk equals a clear mind!"* you tell yourself as the Big Scary Task lurks in the background, waiting to pounce.

But why do we love busy work so much? Simple: it's easy and safe. There's no risk of failure when you're sharpening pencils or clearing notifications from your phone. These tasks are quick, rewarding, and come with a sense of accomplishment—even if you're just completing the low-hanging fruit of your to-do list. It feels productive without requiring you to face the more complex, daunting work that actually matters.

Of course, busy work isn't inherently bad. It can help you ease into the day, build momentum, or provide a mental break. The trouble starts when it takes over, filling your time and leaving no room for what's important. (Let's face it: color-coding your spice rack is probably not the key to career success.)

The first step to taming your busy-work habit is identifying it. Ask yourself, *"Am I working on something that truly moves the needle?"* Be honest. Checking off a bunch of tiny, low-priority tasks might feel satisfying, but if they're not contributing to your actual goals, they're just shiny distractions. And no, alphabetizing your stationery drawer does not count as "essential prep" for writing a report.

To break free, try the *One Big Thing* approach. Each day, choose one important task to focus on. That doesn't mean you can't do anything else, but your priority is chipping away at the Big Scary Task. This method prevents you from filling your day with low-stakes busy work while your critical projects languish.

Another strategy is to use busy work as a reward, not a default. Tell yourself, *"Once I finish 30 minutes of focused work on this project, I'll spend 10 minutes clearing my inbox."* This reframes busy work as a well-earned break instead of a sneaky way to avoid real work. It's still satisfying, but now it serves your productivity rather than derailing it.

Timers can also help. Set a timer for 20 minutes and dedicate that block exclusively to your high-priority task. When the timer goes off, give yourself permission to tackle some busy work—reorganize your desk, file papers, or update your calendar. This balance keeps you productive while ensuring that busy work doesn't monopolize your day.

One of the most powerful tools for combating busy-work procrastination is prioritization. Divide your tasks into categories: high-priority (must-do), medium-priority (nice-to-do), and low-priority (can-wait). When you see how little time you're spending on high-priority items, it's a wake-up call to adjust your focus. Sure, answering emails feels productive, but will it help you finish the presentation that's due tomorrow? Probably not.

And let's not forget humor. Busy work can be hilariously ridiculous when you see it for what it is. Reorganizing your fridge or cleaning your keyboard with a toothpick isn't *wrong*—it's just not the heroic feat of productivity you're pretending it is. Laughing at yourself is a great way to snap out of the busy-work trance and refocus on what matters.

Busy-Work Procrastinators, your ability to tackle the unnecessary is impressive, but don't let it overshadow the important. A little busy work here and there? Totally fine. But remember, the real magic happens when you channel your energy into the tasks that truly matter. Because as satisfying as a spotless desk might be, it's nothing compared to the satisfaction of conquering that Big Scary Task.

How to Use Each Style Productively with Humor and Awareness

Now that you've identified your procrastination persona—Over-Planner, Daydreamer, or Busy-Work Procrastinator—it's time to do the impossible: make these habits work for you. Yes, it's true. Even the quirkiest procrastination styles can be harnessed for productivity with a little humor, self-awareness, and a lot of patience. So, let's take a closer look at how to turn your particular flavor of avoidance into a tool for progress.

First up, Over-Planners. You love a good system, a detailed spreadsheet, and a color-coded timeline. You're the type to plan your grocery list by aisle and category, which is impressive but unnecessary when you're buying five items. The key to productivity for Over-Planners is learning when to stop planning and start doing. Here's a trick: instead of making a perfect, multi-step plan, create what we'll call a *"lazy plan."* It's a simple outline with just enough structure to get you started. Think of it as planning's laid-back cousin—low-pressure and chill. Once you're rolling, you can tweak your system as needed. After all, what good is a flawless plan if you never execute it?

For Daydreamers, your imagination is your superpower—but let's admit it, you've probably spent more time designing fantasy theme parks in your head than on your actual projects. The key here is balance. Instead of letting your ideas float away like balloons at a birthday party, start grounding them. Use tools like a notebook, voice memos, or a sketchpad to capture your brilliant flashes of inspiration. Then, choose *one* idea to act on. (No, you can't do them all at once. Sorry.) Even if it's a small step, like googling how to start a theme park, it's a step forward. Just remember, you can't ride the Ferris wheel of your imagination forever—eventually, you have to buy some tickets.

And now, Busy-Work Procrastinators. Oh, how you love the satisfaction of low-stakes victories. You've probably crossed "write to-do list" off your to-do list more times than you care to admit. The key for you is using busy work strategically, not as an escape hatch. Pair your busy work with meaningful tasks: "Answer these five emails *after* writing the first paragraph of my report." Make busy work your carrot, not your cart. And for the love of sticky notes, stop dusting things that aren't dusty. You've done enough.

Regardless of your style, the ultimate hack is awareness. Recognize when your procrastination tendencies are sneaking in, and gently redirect yourself. Over-Planners ask, *"Am I planning or just avoiding?"* Daydreamers, try, *"Is this idea leading to action?"* Busy workers, get real: *"Is this task actually important?"* Awareness doesn't mean you'll never fall into old habits—it just means you'll catch yourself sooner and laugh about it.

Speaking of laughter, don't take this process too seriously. Productivity doesn't have to be grim or joyless. The more you can laugh at your procrastination quirks, the easier they are to manage. If you find yourself spending an hour reorganizing your spice rack instead of starting your presentation, congratulate yourself on having the best-labeled paprika in town and then get back to work. A little humor goes a long way.

The beauty of understanding your procrastination style is that it gives you tools to navigate your tendencies instead of battling them. You're not trying to *fix* yourself—you're just learning how to work with what you've got. And when you do, you might just find that your procrastination quirks are less of a hindrance and more of an asset.

As we wrap up this chapter, take a moment to appreciate the ridiculousness and brilliance of your procrastination style. Whether you're drowning in sticky notes, lost in a daydream, or triumphantly scrubbing an already clean sink, you're not alone—and you're not beyond hope. The key to success is finding ways to make procrastination productive. And sometimes, all it takes is a fresh perspective—or a clever little strategy to trick yourself into action.

TWO

Mastering the Art of "Intentional" Procrastination

Procrastination gets a bad reputation, but let's be real—it's not all bad. In fact, when done right, it can be an art form. Think about it: some of history's greatest ideas probably came to life while someone was avoiding something else. Who invented fire? Probably someone who didn't feel like gathering berries. Procrastination isn't laziness—it's your brain saying, *"Let's take the scenic route to productivity."*

But there's a fine line between intentional procrastination and, well, binge-watching an entire season of your favorite show while your deadlines glare at you from across the room. That's where this chapter comes in. Instead of letting procrastination control you, why not make it work for you? Enter the world of *intentional* procrastination—a strategy that lets you embrace your natural tendencies while still making progress. Yes, you can procrastinate *on purpose* and still get things done. (Mind-blowing, right?)

We're going to explore how to use procrastination as a tool instead of a trap. From turning distractions into productive breaks to structuring your avoidance with actual purpose, you'll learn how to procrastinate like a pro. No more guilt-ridden scroll-a-thons—just strategically placed pauses that fuel creativity, recharge your brain, and maybe even make you more productive in the long run.

So, grab your half-finished to-do list, take a deep breath, and let's dive in. You're about to discover that procrastination isn't the villain of your productivity story—it's the quirky sidekick you never knew you needed.

How to Make Procrastination Work for You Rather Than Against You

Procrastination isn't laziness—it's a misunderstood art form. Done wrong, it leaves you binge-watching shows while deadlines glare at you from across the room. But done right? It's a secret weapon for creativity and productivity. The trick is making procrastination work *for you*, not against you. Yes, it's possible. Let's dive in.

First, reframe procrastination as thinking time. When you delay a task, your subconscious gets to work. Ever notice how your best ideas strike while you're showering or, embarrassingly, mid-scroll through cat memes? That's not a coincidence—it's your brain connecting dots while you're busy *not* stressing over the task. Instead of fighting this, embrace it. Let procrastination simmer in the background while you "research" the perfect home office plants on Pinterest.

Now, meet your new best friend: **structured procrastination.** Coined by philosopher John Perry, this concept involves avoiding one daunting task by doing another, less-intimidating one. Say you're procrastinating on writing a report. Instead, you decide to clean your desk. Did you finish the report? Nope. But now your desk is spotless, and the workspace feels more inviting. You procrastinated, but you also got something useful done. That's what we call a win-win.

Deadlines are procrastination's personal trainers—they push you to perform when you'd rather be anywhere else. But here's the trick: set fake deadlines. If your actual deadline is Friday, tell yourself it's Tuesday. Your brain doesn't need to know the truth. That last-minute adrenaline rush? It'll kick in on your fake deadline, leaving the real one as a bonus buffer. It's the procrastinator's version of time travel.

Next, let's talk about "productive procrastination." When you're avoiding a task, use that time to prepare for it. Not ready to write the presentation? Fine. Brainstorm ideas, sketch an outline, or pick a killer font for your slides. You're still not tackling the Big Scary Task, but you're warming up for it. Think of it like stretching before a workout—low effort, but critical to success.

Intentional breaks are another powerful tool. Don't let distractions ambush you—schedule them. Yes, schedule procrastination. Block out 15 minutes to scroll, snack, or stare out the window guilt-free. Knowing you have a planned pause makes it easier to focus during work sessions. Plus, procrastination is way more fun when it's officially on your calendar. Who doesn't love a sanctioned snack break?

Procrastination can also help you prioritize. Delay something long enough, and you'll discover which tasks truly matter. If the world doesn't implode because you didn't reply to that email, maybe it wasn't urgent after all. Strategic procrastination helps you filter out unnecessary clutter, leaving you to focus on the tasks that actually move the needle.

Of course, this only works if you keep procrastination in check. Set limits. Use timers to corral your avoidance into manageable bursts. For example, dedicate 20 minutes to your main task and then reward yourself with five minutes of procrastination—like folding laundry or googling "how to train a hamster to fetch coffee." By balancing work and breaks, you stay productive without spiraling into full-on avoidance.

Humor is your ultimate ally here. When you catch yourself organizing your closet instead of tackling a deadline, don't beat yourself up. Laugh at the absurdity. Self-awareness is the secret sauce of successful procrastinators. The more you can recognize—and poke fun at—your own quirks, the easier it becomes to channel them productively.

The golden rule? Procrastinate with purpose. It's not about avoiding work entirely—it's about redirecting that avoidance into something meaningful. Whether you're clearing clutter, brainstorming, or taking a break, you're still moving forward, even if it's sideways.

So, the next time you find yourself procrastinating, don't panic. Take a breath, grab a timer, and use it to your advantage. After all, procrastinators always seem to pull it off at the last minute—and with the right mindset, you can too. Progress doesn't have to be perfect—it just has to start.

The Benefits of "Structured" Procrastination as Part of Productivity

Procrastination often gets labeled as the villain of productivity, but what if it could be the hero in disguise? Enter *structured procrastination,* the art of avoiding your most pressing task by doing something else useful. It's procrastination with a purpose—a way to delay without guilt and still feel accomplished. Think of it as the productivity version of ordering dessert before dinner. Sure, it's unconventional, but it works.

Here's how it goes: instead of tackling the Big Scary Task staring you down, you focus on smaller, manageable tasks that have been lingering on your to-do list. You're still procrastinating, but you're also making progress elsewhere. Say you're avoiding writing a report. Rather than doom-scrolling on your phone, you decide to clean your desk. Did you finish the report? Nope. But now you have a pristine workspace that practically begs you to sit down and write. That's the magic of structured procrastination—you're productive, just not in the way you expected.

Why does this work? Because structured procrastination turns avoidance into action. The looming deadline of your Big Task creates a sense of urgency that spills over into smaller, less intimidating tasks. Suddenly, the things you've been putting off for weeks—organizing your email inbox, fixing the squeaky cabinet door, or finally changing the lightbulb in your closet—become appealing. It's procrastination with a side of accomplishment.

Another perk is that it keeps your brain engaged without overwhelming it. Working on low-stakes tasks gives your mind a chance to recharge while still feeling productive. You might even find that while you're alphabetizing your spice rack, inspiration strikes for that report introduction. It's like your brain sneaks off to work on the real problem while you're busy elsewhere.

Structured procrastination also redefines boring chores as satisfying victories. Filing old receipts, clearing out your junk drawer, or updating your LinkedIn profile suddenly feels purposeful when it's replacing something more daunting. You're still working, just on tasks that feel doable in the moment. It's procrastination logic at its finest: *"Sure, I didn't write my novel, but my inbox is at zero, so I'm basically a productivity guru."*

What's even better? Structured procrastination builds momentum. Once you've conquered a few smaller tasks, you start to feel unstoppable. That sense of accomplishment often carries over into your Big Task. By the time you've rearranged your bookshelf and wondered why you own three copies of the same book, you're ready to face the bigger challenge. Who knew organizing could be your gateway to progress?

But let's set some boundaries here. Structured procrastination isn't about spending six hours deep-cleaning your house while your deadline inches closer. It works best with a time limit or a preselected list of "acceptable" tasks. Think of things like replying to emails, tidying your desk, or prepping for tomorrow's dinner—quick wins that don't devour your entire day. Set a timer if you have to. Nothing kills procrastination joy faster than realizing you've spent three hours deciding which socks spark joy.

Let's also acknowledge the humor in all of this. There's something delightfully absurd about vacuuming your curtains instead of writing a business proposal. When you catch yourself swapping priorities, embrace the ridiculousness. Structured procrastination is as much about tricking your brain as it is about getting things done. Laughing at your procrastination quirks makes the process feel lighter and more manageable.

At its core, structured procrastination is about turning your natural avoidance tendencies into something useful. You're not ignoring the Big Task forever—you're just warming up. By the end of the day, the Big Scary Task will still be waiting for you, but you'll have knocked out so many smaller jobs that you'll feel ready to tackle it.

So, the next time you're tempted to avoid something important, don't fight it—channel it. Use structured procrastination to clean, organize, or brainstorm your way into productivity. And once you've mastered that, you'll see that even your breaks and distractions can supercharge your workflow in ways you never expected.

Turning Breaks and Distractions into Intentional Recharges

Procrastination's sneakiest accomplice is distraction. One moment you're ready to conquer your to-do list, and the next, you're watching a video on how to train squirrels to play fetch. But here's the secret: distractions don't have to derail you. In fact, when handled with purpose, they can recharge your brain and even boost productivity. Yes, your random rabbit holes might just have a higher calling.

Let's talk about breaks first. If your idea of productivity is working nonstop until you collapse into a heap, congratulations—you've mastered the art of burnout. Your brain isn't a machine; it's more like a whiny toddler. It needs regular rest, or it'll throw a tantrum. Intentional breaks—short, planned pauses—are your brain's snack time, giving it the energy it needs to focus again.

Not all breaks are created equal, though. The difference between "I'm taking a 10-minute stretch" and "I'm watching a quick video" can be the difference between refocusing and spiraling into three hours of conspiracy theories about how dinosaurs built the pyramids. The key is to set boundaries. Use a timer to keep your breaks from becoming full-on distractions. It might feel silly to set a five-minute alarm for pacing around your living room, but it's better than accidentally deep-cleaning your entire house just to avoid one email.

Speaking of distractions, let's address their bad reputation. They're not always the villains of productivity. Your brain loves variety, and short distractions can give it a mental reset. The trick is to turn distractions into something intentional—or at least something that doesn't involve creating a new Pinterest board for "holiday llama decor" when your deadline is tomorrow.

One way to manage distractions is to treat them as rewards. For example, after 30 minutes of focused work, give yourself five minutes to indulge in whatever has been tempting you. Want to scroll through memes? Go for it—but use a timer so you don't get sucked in. This approach transforms distractions from guilt-inducing time-wasters into mini celebrations of progress. Plus, knowing you have a scheduled break coming up makes it easier to stay focused during your work sessions.

Another strategy is to make your distractions slightly productive. If you're avoiding a task, pick a distraction that serves a purpose. For instance, if you're stuck on a project, take a "distraction walk" while brainstorming solutions. Or, if you're itching to clean, focus on an area that genuinely needs attention—like your desk instead of your already-pristine bookshelf. This way, your distractions feel less like avoidance and more like multitasking genius.

And then there's the magic of creative distractions. Sometimes, stepping away to doodle, bake, or reorganize a drawer can spark fresh ideas. Ever notice how your best ideas hit you while you're in the shower or folding laundry? That's your brain quietly solving problems in the background while you're distracted. Lean into that process, and give yourself permission to do something unrelated— just don't forget to come back.

The goal here is balance. Intentional breaks and mindful distractions let you recharge without losing sight of your goals. Think of them as pit stops in a race. Without them, you're running on fumes. With them, you're refueled and ready to zoom ahead. The key is to keep those pit stops brief and purposeful so they don't turn into all-day detours.

Of course, there's humor in this journey. If you catch yourself alphabetizing your spice rack instead of writing a report, don't panic. Laugh at your procrastination quirk, reset, and move on. Distractions are inevitable, but learning to manage them makes all the difference. With practice, you'll stop feeling guilty about those little detours and start using them to your advantage.

By embracing breaks and distractions as tools rather than obstacles, you'll find they're not the enemy—they're just misunderstood. Use them wisely, and you'll recharge your brain, boost your focus, and avoid burnout. And once you've mastered the art of intentional pauses, you'll be ready to tackle a whole new level of procrastination power—one that involves planning your procrastination like a true professional.

Lighthearted Reminders That Rest and Creativity Can Benefit Your Work

Let's face it: somewhere along the way, "rest" became a four-letter word in the productivity world. Hustle culture makes us feel like every second not spent grinding away is a failure. But here's a little secret: rest isn't laziness—it's fuel. And when paired with creativity, it becomes the magic sauce that transforms your work from "meh" to "wow." So, let's break down why taking a break and letting your creative side roam free can actually make you more productive.

First, let's talk about rest. Your brain is not a marathon runner—it's more like a sprinter with the attention span of a goldfish. You can't expect it to perform well for hours on end without a break. Research backs this up: regular breaks can improve focus, memory, and overall performance. But here's the fun part: you don't have to feel guilty about them. Rest is like rebooting your mental operating system. Without it, you're basically that one computer from 1998, making strange noises and threatening to crash.

Think of rest as "strategic idleness." Instead of powering through until your brain feels like a foggy mess, step away and recharge. This could mean taking a walk, grabbing a snack, or doing something completely unrelated to work, like staring out the window and pretending you're the main character in a drama. These mini-breaks might feel indulgent, but they're not—they're part of the process. A rested brain is a productive brain.

Now, onto creativity. When was the last time you let yourself do something fun and pointless? And no, scrolling Instagram doesn't count. We're talking real, hands-on creativity: doodling, playing an instrument, or building a model spaceship out of paperclips. Tapping into your creative side isn't just about having fun—it's a sneaky way to give your brain the space it needs to come up with brilliant ideas.

You see when you engage in creative activities, your mind wanders, and that wandering is where the magic happens. Ever notice how your best ideas come to you when you're doing something totally unrelated, like showering or chopping vegetables? That's because creativity thrives in those quiet, unstructured moments. It's like your brain saying, *"Finally! Now that you're not obsessing over that email, I can get to work."*

Not convinced? Here's an example: Beethoven was known for taking long walks in nature, where he came up with many of his musical masterpieces. And let's not forget Einstein, who famously solved problems while playing his violin. If it worked for them, surely you can justify a 20-minute break to sketch terrible cartoons or build a house of cards.

The trick is to let go of the pressure to be good at it. This isn't about creating a masterpiece—it's about freeing your mind from rigid focus and letting it play. Color outside the lines, write a poem that makes no sense or sculpt a vaguely potato-shaped blob and call it modern art. The goal isn't perfection; it's permission.

Here's the kicker: rest and creativity work hand in hand. When you're stuck on a problem, sometimes the best thing you can do is step away and do something completely different. Give your brain a chance to reset, and it might surprise you with a solution that feels effortless. It's like sneaking a cheat code into your productivity game.

But let's keep it light. Don't turn "rest" and "creativity" into new items on your to-do list. This isn't about maximizing every second of your day—it's about giving yourself room to breathe. Laugh at the ridiculousness of your doodles. Enjoy the absurdity of creating origami that looks nothing like a swan. And if anyone questions why you're knitting a scarf instead of writing a report, just tell them you're channeling your inner Einstein.

In the end, rest and creativity aren't indulgences—they're investments in your productivity. A brain that's rested and recharged is a brain that can tackle anything, even that Big Scary Task you've been avoiding. And once you've mastered the art of recharging with purpose, it's time to take things up a notch and build a procrastination schedule that works with your natural rhythms, not against them. Stay tuned.

THREE

Productive Procrastination Tasks (If You're Not Ready to Dive In)

Procrastination isn't always about doing *nothing*. Sometimes, it's about doing absolutely *everything else* that isn't the thing you're supposed to be doing. And you know what? That's not all bad. Welcome to productive procrastination: the ultimate guilt-free way to avoid work while still looking like you've got it all together. Think of it as the equivalent of rearranging your fridge before starting a diet—it's not the main event, but it's technically progress.

This chapter is all about finding those sweet, low-pressure tasks that make you feel like you're winning at life, even if you're strategically dodging your Big Scary Task. From tidying up your workspace to ticking off the tiniest wins on your to-do list, these activities are designed to make procrastination feel a little less like avoiding and a little more like prepping. So, grab your favorite distraction and let's turn procrastination into a productivity loophole.

Organizing Your Workspace or Clearing Digital Clutter

Procrastination is like a messy desk—it gets in the way, and eventually, you just can't ignore it anymore. But here's the trick: instead of diving straight into your Big Scary Task, you can ease into productivity by tidying up your space or clearing out that jungle of digital clutter you've been avoiding for approximately forever. It's productive procrastination at its finest because even though you're technically avoiding work, you're still setting yourself up for success. Bonus: it feels way more satisfying than staring blankly at a to-do list.

Let's start with your physical workspace. Take a look around. Is your desk a cluttered disaster of papers, pens, coffee mugs, and that one charger you swear belongs to *something*? Great! This is your chance to procrastinate with purpose. Grab a trash can, start sorting, and pretend you're on one of those home makeover shows. Toss what you don't need (bye, random Post-its), organize what you do, and give everything a proper place. You're not just tidying—you're creating a productivity sanctuary where magic (or at least mediocre effort) can happen.

Once you've tackled your desk, turn your attention to the digital chaos. If your computer desktop looks like a game of "guess which file is important," it's time for some folder feng shui. Start by dragging everything into a folder labeled "To Sort Later." Is this actual sorting? No. Does it make your desktop look clean in under 10 seconds? Absolutely. From there, create subfolders for the essentials —work projects, personal files, and that "Random Stuff" folder you'll never fully deal with but can't bring yourself to delete.

Don't stop at your desktop—your email inbox is begging for attention. If you've got unread messages in the triple digits (or worse, quadruple), this is your time to shine. Start with the obvious spam and newsletters you don't care about. Then, set up filters for the emails you want to keep but don't need to see immediately. By the time you're done, your inbox will be as close to zero as it's been since the dawn of Gmail. Plus, cleaning out your inbox feels like real productivity, even though you're just avoiding the harder stuff.

If email isn't your jam, tackle your phone. How many apps do you have that you haven't opened since downloading? (Looking at you, random fitness tracker from 2019.) Delete the ones you don't use, organize the ones you do into folders, and maybe even update your wallpaper for a fresh vibe. Sure, it's procrastination, but it's *aesthetic* procrastination, which is practically an achievement in itself.

And let's not forget the joy of untangling physical clutter in other corners of your life. That junk drawer? Pure procrastination gold. Dive into the chaos, marvel at the random batteries, old keys, and three pairs of scissors you don't remember buying, and emerge victorious with a drawer that actually closes. Or tackle your bookshelf—whether you alphabetize it, arrange it by color, or group it by the likelihood of ever reading the books, the satisfaction is unbeatable.

The best part about organizing and decluttering is that it gives you an excuse to not work *and* makes you feel productive at the same time. It's like tricking your brain into thinking, *"Wow, I'm accomplishing so much,"* while your actual deadlines laugh quietly in the corner. Plus, when you finally get around to the real work, you'll have a clean, organized environment that practically begs for focus.

But don't get carried away. Organizing is a means to an end, not an all-day event. If you find yourself three hours into labeling cables by function, it's time to rein it in. Remember, the goal is to use organizing as a warm-up, not as a marathon to avoid your Big Scary Task entirely.

So, grab a trash bag, dust off your files, and get to work... on avoiding actual work. Who knows? By the time your desk is spotless and your inbox is cleared, you might just feel ready to take on the world—or at least one of the less-terrifying items on your to-do list. And if not? Well, there's always the joy of organizing your sock drawer.

Creative Brainstorming Sessions to Procrastinate Without Guilt

If procrastination were an art form, brainstorming would be its boldest brushstroke. Nothing feels quite as satisfying as sitting down to "work" and instead spiraling into a whirlwind of creative ideas that, let's be honest, you may or may not ever use. But here's the beauty of it: brainstorming is a productive way to procrastinate. You're not avoiding work—you're generating *ideas.* Big ideas, small ideas, wild ideas that involve jetpacks and alpacas. It doesn't matter if they're immediately useful, because brainstorming makes you feel busy while technically accomplishing... something.

The first rule of procrastination-friendly brainstorming is to lower the stakes. This isn't about creating a perfect plan or solving world hunger—it's about giving your brain permission to wander freely without the pressure of immediate results. Grab a notebook, a whiteboard, or even a stack of sticky notes and let your imagination run wild. No idea is too ridiculous during this stage. Want to revolutionize the way humans use zippers? Go for it. Considering opening a themed restaurant where all the food is shaped like hedgehogs? Write it down. You never know which spark of nonsense might lead to brilliance.

Not sure how to start? Use prompts to kick things off. Try "What's the most absurd way to solve this problem?" or "If I had infinite time and money, what would I do?" These kinds of questions are like open invitations for your brain to stop overthinking and just play. Remember, brainstorming is your free pass to dream big without judgment. Nobody's grading your ideas here, so if your solution to your project involves building a time machine, embrace it.

If solo brainstorming feels too lonely, bring in a partner. Sometimes, bouncing ideas off someone else can turn your procrastination into a full-on creative jam session. Warning: this can be dangerously fun, so set a timer if you don't want to spend two hours debating whether penguins would make good service animals. (Spoiler: they wouldn't. But the conversation is worth having.)

For visual thinkers, mind mapping is a fantastic way to capture ideas. Start with your main topic in the center of the page, then branch out with related thoughts, subcategories, and absurd tangents that make you laugh. Use different colors, doodles, or symbols to keep it lively. This is brainstorming, not corporate accounting, so feel free to get messy. The chaos might just inspire your next big idea.

And don't limit yourself to work-related brainstorming. Use this time to think about personal projects you've been putting off, like planning your dream vacation, creating a home garden, or finally figuring out how to organize your closet so it doesn't look like a tornado hit it. Brainstorming doesn't have to be about productivity —it can simply be about exploring your creativity and giving your brain a fun little detour.

Of course, the real magic of brainstorming comes from occasionally acting on your ideas. Pick one idea—just one—and take a small step toward making it real. Maybe it's jotting down an outline, sketching a rough draft, or doing five minutes of research. Turning even one brainstorming session into action reminds you that all those creative detours weren't just for show—they were the first steps toward something cool.

The best part of brainstorming is how sneaky it is. You're procrastinating, but you're also generating ideas, solving problems, and maybe even sparking a little inspiration for the task you were avoiding. Who knew putting off work could feel so productive?

So, the next time you're staring down a task you're not ready to tackle, grab a pen, set a timer, and let your mind wander. Whether you're solving the world's biggest challenges or just deciding how to turn your living room into a jungle-themed oasis, brainstorming is the ultimate guilt-free procrastination. And hey, if none of it works out, at least you've got some killer ideas for your memoir, *"How I Avoided Work and Accidentally Changed the World."*

Finding "Tiny Wins" in Your To-Do List to Gain Momentum

Procrastination doesn't have to mean doing nothing. Sometimes, it's about finding small, achievable tasks—"tiny wins"—that give you a much-needed sense of accomplishment while the Big Scary Task lurks in the corner. Tiny wins are like the appetizers of productivity: they won't fill you up, but they'll give you just enough motivation to keep going.

The genius of tiny wins lies in their simplicity. They're quick, low-pressure, and oddly satisfying. Think about tasks that take two minutes or less, like responding to an email, watering your plants, or finally tossing out that dried-up pen you've been keeping for no reason. Are these tasks life-changing? No. But do they count as progress? Absolutely.

Here's the magic: every tiny win gives your brain a small hit of dopamine. That little rush of accomplishment makes you feel capable, which often carries over into tackling more intimidating work. It's like starting a workout with stretches—not the main event, but enough to get your momentum going.

To get started, grab your to-do list—or make one if it doesn't exist yet (congratulations, that's your first win). Look for tasks that are so easy you'll wonder if they even count as work. Examples include:

- Deleting five junk emails.

- Wiping crumbs off your desk.
- Writing a single sentence of the report you've been dreading.
- Scheduling an appointment you've been putting off.

The point is to build momentum, not stress yourself out. When you complete one small task, you're setting off a chain reaction. Suddenly, you're not just deleting emails—you're clearing your inbox. You're not just wiping crumbs—you're tidying your whole desk. Each tiny win boosts your confidence and makes the next step feel less daunting.

Tiny wins are also great for procrastinators who love avoiding the Big Scary Task by "preparing." Let's say you're putting off a high-stakes project. Instead of diving in, fix the formatting on one slide. Tweak the font. Then, maybe—just maybe—you'll feel ready to tackle the substance. It's a sneaky way to trick your brain into easing into the bigger work.

But let's be honest—tiny wins are addictive. Is there anything more satisfying than crossing something off your list? Even if it's as minor as "replace batteries in remote," that big, bold checkmark feels like a trophy. But don't let the pursuit of tiny wins derail your day. If you've spent two hours reorganizing your bookshelf instead of writing a report, you've gone from productive procrastination to full-blown avoidance.

To avoid falling into the tiny-win trap, set a time limit. Dedicate 15–30 minutes to knocking out small tasks and then transition to something more substantial. Use tiny wins as a warm-up, not the whole workout. They're there to build confidence, not replace the important stuff entirely.

Another strategy is to celebrate your wins—no matter how small. Did you finally untangle those ancient headphones? Clap for yourself. Found the mystery smell in the fridge and dealt with it? Do a victory dance. Recognizing these tiny accomplishments reinforces the idea that progress, however small, is still progress.

Tiny wins are especially helpful when you're feeling stuck or overwhelmed. When the Big Scary Task feels like too much to handle, focusing on something small reminds you that action is possible. You might not be ready to write the entire report, but you can write the title. You might not have the energy to clean the whole house, but you can clear off the coffee table. Progress is progress, no matter how small.

Ultimately, tiny wins are about building momentum. They're proof that even small actions can lead to big results. By focusing on what you *can* do instead of what feels impossible, you'll find yourself inching closer to tackling the things that matter most. And who knows? By the time you've crossed off a few wins, that Big Scary Task might not seem so scary anymore. Or, at the very least, your desk will be spotless, your inbox will be clear, and you'll feel ready to face the day.

Humor About Feeling Accomplished from Small, Easy Tasks

There's nothing quite like crossing a task off your to-do list, especially when the task is so simple it shouldn't even count. Drank water? Productivity champ. Sent a "Thanks!" email? You're practically the CEO of Getting Things Done, Inc. These "tiny wins" are the bread and butter of procrastination mastery—they're quick, satisfying, and give you a sense of accomplishment without requiring much effort. For procrastinators, they're the equivalent of warming up before a marathon. You're not running the race yet, but at least you've tied your shoes.

Tiny wins work because they trick your brain into thinking you're unstoppable. Completing even the smallest task—like deleting junk emails or wiping crumbs off your desk—gives you a dopamine boost, that little rush of, *"Look at me, I'm crushing it!"* That sense of achievement builds momentum, making it easier to tackle the next thing on your list. The beauty of tiny wins is that they're so easy you'd have to go out of your way to fail. Finally put away your coffee mug? Boom, you're a productivity wizard.

Of course, not all tiny wins are created equal. Some are genuinely helpful, like organizing your workspace or jotting down a rough outline for your project. Others are hilariously low stakes. Alphabetizing your spice rack might not make a dent in your deadline, but for five glorious minutes, you feel like the most organized person in the world. These little victories are the ultimate form of productive procrastination: they're not getting the Big Scary Task done, but they're making you feel like you're moving forward.

One of the funniest aspects of tiny wins is how much we celebrate them. Have you ever written something on your to-do list that you already did, just so you could cross it off? Of course you have—everyone has. There's no greater thrill than adding "wake up" or "drink coffee" to your list and immediately marking it complete. It's the equivalent of giving yourself a participation trophy for existing, and honestly, you deserve it.

But tiny wins are more than just a procrastinator's excuse—they're a way to build confidence. When you're staring down a mountain of work, it's easy to feel overwhelmed. Small victories remind you that progress doesn't have to be monumental to matter. Folding laundry or replying to an email might not seem like much, but it's action. And action, no matter how small, is what gets you unstuck.

These wins also serve as a mental warm-up. Let's say you're avoiding a massive report. Instead of diving in headfirst, you start by fixing the formatting on one slide. Then you tweak the title font. Before you know it, you're adjusting bullet points and writing sentences. What felt impossible an hour ago suddenly seems manageable, all because you eased into it with tiny, low-pressure tasks.

However, there's a fine line between productive procrastination and full-blown avoidance. If you've spent two hours organizing your desk accessories instead of doing actual work, it might be time to reassess. Tiny wins are supposed to pave the way for bigger tasks, not become an endless loop of pencil sharpening and paperclip counting. To keep things balanced, set a timer for 15–30 minutes of small tasks, then transition to something more substantial.

The key to tiny wins is embracing their humor and simplicity. Did you finally delete an app you haven't used since 2019? Clap for yourself. Paired all your socks? That's Nobel Prize-level achievement in the world of procrastination. Laugh at how silly it feels to celebrate these moments, but don't discount their value. They're the building blocks of progress, no matter how small.

Small wins are powerful, but they're not the whole picture. To truly make procrastination work for you, you need more than a handful of quick tasks—you need a system that builds on these victories. A flexible schedule that makes room for procrastination, breaks, and bursts of brilliance is the next step. The next chapter explores how to make a plan that works with your quirks, not against them.

FOUR

Creating a Flexible Procrastination Schedule

Schedules are supposed to be the ultimate tool for productivity, but for procrastinators, they often feel like a cruel joke. A rigid timetable? Please. That's just a fancy way of saying, "Here's a list of things you'll definitely avoid today." But what if your schedule could embrace your procrastination habits instead of fighting against them? What if, instead of guilt-tripping you, it worked with your natural tendencies to help you get things done—at your own pace?

Welcome to the world of flexible procrastination scheduling. It's not about forcing yourself to stick to an unrealistic plan or pretending you're someone who thrives on rigidity. Instead, it's about building a schedule that gives you structure without suffocating you, one that leaves room for breaks, distractions, and those inevitable moments of *"I just can't right now."* In this chapter, we'll explore how to create a procrastination-friendly schedule that keeps you on track while still letting you be, well... you. Because the secret to productivity isn't perfection—it's finding a system that works for your unique chaos.

Building Time Buffers to Allow for Procrastination Without Stress

Let's face it—procrastination happens. No matter how ambitious you are when you plan your day, there's always that moment when your brain says, *"Nope, not now,"* and suddenly you're deep into a YouTube rabbit hole on "How to Train Your Pet Goldfish" instead of tackling your project. The trick isn't to eliminate procrastination (good luck with that)—it's to plan for it. Enter **time buffers**: little pockets of extra time you build into your schedule to handle the inevitable distractions, delays, and mental detours that life throws your way.

Time buffers are like the airbags of your productivity. Without them, one hiccup—like an unexpected phone call or a snack break that turns into a full-blown grazing session—can send your whole day off track. But with them? You have room to procrastinate without derailing your entire schedule. Think of it as procrastination insurance. Sure, it doesn't stop you from avoiding tasks, but it does protect your day from total chaos.

The first step to creating time buffers is to accept a basic truth: you're not a robot. Most of us dramatically underestimate how long things take. (*"Oh, I can totally write that report in an hour!"*) Spoiler alert: you can't. To make your schedule realistic, add some cushion time to everything. If you think a task will take 30 minutes, schedule 45. That way, when you inevitably get distracted—or spend five minutes overthinking your email salutation—you're not throwing off the entire day.

Buffers are also essential between tasks. Have you ever planned back-to-back meetings or tried to go straight from one major project to another? Yeah, that never works. Instead, you end up taking an unplanned "break" that eats into your next task. By building in 15–30 minutes of buffer time between appointments or big jobs, you give yourself room to breathe, refocus, or, yes, procrastinate just a little.

One of the best procrastination-proofing tools is **the magic hour**—a dedicated block of time at the end of the day for catching up on whatever you didn't finish. Think of it as your "oops, I got distracted" safety net. Did you spend half the afternoon rearranging your bookshelf instead of answering emails? No worries. The magic hour lets you handle leftover tasks without stress. Knowing you have this time also reduces the pressure to be perfect all day, making it easier to stay calm and focused.

Time buffers are especially useful for creative projects. Let's be honest: creativity has its own schedule. You can't just sit down and demand brilliant ideas to appear. Sometimes you need to doodle, stare at the ceiling, or take an extended snack break before inspiration strikes. Adding extra time to creative work gives your brain permission to wander and recharge, which often leads to better results anyway.

Another way buffers save the day is by preparing you for the unexpected. Life happens—your internet goes out, your neighbor decides now is the perfect time to practice their drum solo, or you accidentally spend 30 minutes researching why flamingos stand on one leg. These distractions are inevitable, but with a little extra time built in, they won't ruin your day. And if everything goes smoothly? That buffer time becomes bonus free time for you to enjoy guilt-free.

Of course, time buffers only work if you don't abuse them. They're not an excuse to procrastinate endlessly (*"Well, I blocked out an hour for 'research,' so obviously I need to watch 14 cat videos..."*). Instead, think of them as safety nets. They give you space to breathe without letting your procrastination take over completely.

Adding time buffers to your schedule isn't about admitting defeat; it's about being realistic. By planning for procrastination, you can work with it rather than against it. Instead of stressing out every time your brain wanders, you'll have the freedom to pause, regroup, and still stay on track. It's not about being perfect—it's about setting yourself up for success, one realistic time block at a time.

Setting Realistic Daily Goals and Pacing Yourself with Breaks

Let's be honest: when it comes to setting daily goals, most of us are a little too ambitious. You wake up, sip your coffee, and confidently write a to-do list long enough to make a productivity coach cry tears of pride. Then by 5 PM, you've crossed off two things, half-heartedly started a third, and spent an hour deciding which font to use for your calendar app. The problem? Your goals weren't realistic—and by "realistic," I mean "actually achievable by a single human in one day."

Setting realistic daily goals isn't just about managing your time; it's about managing your expectations. The first step is to accept that you can't do everything. Seriously, you can't. Stop trying to jam 48 hours' worth of tasks into a single day—it's not impressive; it's exhausting. Instead, aim for a *manageable* number of priorities. Think quality over quantity: three to five meaningful tasks are way better than 15 half-finished ones. Sure, it might feel like you're underachieving at first, but spoiler alert: you're not. You're just working smarter, not harder.

Once you've narrowed down your to-do list, it's time to prioritize. Procrastinators love to avoid the Big Scary Task by focusing on low-stakes busywork, like organizing paper clips or replying to emails that didn't need a response. Don't fall for it. Pick one high-priority item —yes, just one—and make it your main focus for the day. That's your "One Big Thing." If you get that done, everything else is gravy.

The beauty of this approach is that it forces you to set realistic expectations for yourself. You're not aiming to conquer the world in one day; you're aiming to tackle *one big thing* and maybe a few smaller ones. This shift in mindset can turn even the most overwhelmed procrastinator into a productivity machine. Or at least a productivity scooter—but hey, progress is progress.

Now, let's talk about pacing yourself. Most procrastinators have two speeds: "do nothing" and "panic mode." Neither is particularly effective. What you need is a middle ground, and that's where pacing comes in. Instead of trying to power through an eight-hour work session (*ha, like that's happening*), break your day into manageable chunks. Work for 25–30 minutes, then take a five-minute break. This method, often called the Pomodoro Technique, is procrastinator-friendly because it turns your tasks into bite-sized pieces. Plus, knowing a break is coming makes it easier to stay focused.

Speaking of breaks, let's make one thing clear: breaks are not the enemy. In fact, they're your secret weapon for avoiding burnout. The key is to make them intentional. Step away from your desk, stretch, grab a snack, or go outside for some fresh air. What you *don't* want to do is fall into the classic procrastinator trap of turning a "quick" break into a 45-minute scroll-a-thon through TikTok. Use a timer if you have to. Breaks should refresh you, not derail you.

Another pacing strategy is to mix easy tasks with hard ones. Start with something manageable to build momentum—like sending a quick email or tidying your desk—then dive into a more challenging task. Think of it as a productivity sandwich: the easy stuff is the bread, and the hard stuff is the meat (or tofu, if that's your vibe). This balance keeps your day from feeling like an uphill slog.

And let's not forget the power of celebrating small wins. Every time you check something off your list, take a moment to acknowledge it. Did you finish your One Big Thing? Amazing! Treat yourself to a guilt-free break. Finished a smaller task? Clap for yourself. No win is too small to celebrate, and those celebrations keep you motivated for the next round.

At the end of the day, setting realistic goals and pacing yourself isn't about working harder—it's about working smarter. You're not trying to defeat procrastination; you're learning to outmaneuver it. With manageable goals, strategic breaks, and a little self-compassion, you can turn even the laziest day into a productive one. And honestly, isn't that the real dream?

Using Timers and Alarms for Structured Work Sessions

For procrastinators, time is a slippery little devil. You sit down with the best intentions to "just check one email," and suddenly it's two hours later, you've fallen down a rabbit hole of trivia about penguins, and your actual work is still untouched. Enter the humble timer— your new best friend in the fight against procrastination. With a simple beep or buzz, it can wrangle your wandering mind and bring some much-needed structure to your day.

Timers and alarms are procrastination-proof because they create boundaries. Instead of diving headfirst into a task with no end in sight (and no clue how long it might take), you set a specific amount of time to work. Whether it's 15 minutes or an hour, that ticking clock turns the task from "infinite abyss of misery" to "temporary challenge I can survive." It's a game-changer.

Let's start with the Pomodoro Technique, a fan favorite for procrastinators everywhere. The idea is simple: work for 25 minutes, then take a five-minute break. Repeat this cycle four times, and then reward yourself with a longer break—maybe 15 or 20 minutes. This method works because it's manageable. Anyone can focus for 25 minutes, even if you're doing something as soul-crushing as filing expense reports. Knowing a break is just around the corner makes it easier to dive in, and those little intervals of rest keep your brain from fizzling out.

If 25 minutes feels too long, don't worry—you can scale it down. Some days, even 15 minutes feels like climbing Mount Everest, and that's okay. Start with five minutes if you need to. Tell yourself, *"I'll just do this for five minutes, and then I can stop."* The funny thing is, once you start, you'll often keep going. The hardest part of any task is starting, and a timer helps you break through that initial resistance.

Timers also shine when it comes to managing breaks. If you're the kind of person who takes a "quick break" that somehow turns into watching three episodes of your favorite show, a timer is your savior. Set it for five or ten minutes, and when it goes off, get back to work. It keeps your downtime from spiraling into a full-blown procrastination binge. Plus, there's something oddly satisfying about hearing that timer beep and thinking, *"Okay, back to it."* It's like having a tiny accountability buddy that lives in your phone or kitchen drawer.

For the ultimate procrastination hack, pair timers with rewards. For example, set a timer for 30 minutes of work and promise yourself a treat at the end—maybe a snack, a quick scroll through social media, or a few minutes of that video game you've been obsessing over. The timer keeps you focused, and the reward gives you something to look forward to. It's the carrot-and-stick approach, but with less stick and more cookies.

Another great use for timers is tackling tasks you dread. Ever feel like something is going to take forever, so you avoid it entirely? A timer can shatter that illusion. Set it for 15 or 20 minutes and see how much you can get done. Chances are, you'll make more progress than you expected, and the task won't seem quite so scary anymore. Plus, knowing the timer will eventually end makes it easier to dive into something unpleasant. You're not committing to eternity—just a few minutes.

If alarms feel more your speed, use them to structure your day. Set reminders for key tasks or transitions, like "start project" or "wrap up break." These nudges help you stay on track without relying solely on willpower. Just be sure to pick a pleasant alarm tone—nobody needs the stress of a blaring siren every hour.

Timers and alarms might seem basic, but don't underestimate their power. They're like tiny, portable productivity coaches, keeping you focused, balanced, and accountable. Whether you're wrangling your workday, managing breaks, or simply trying to avoid an epic procrastination spiral, these tools are a procrastinator's best friend. All it takes is one beep to turn "I'll do it later" into "I'm doing it now."

Embracing the Flow of Productivity with Humor About Flexibility

Productivity often feels like a battle—against distractions, procrastination, and that little voice in your head saying, *"But wouldn't it be more fun to organize your sock drawer?"* But what if productivity didn't have to be so rigid? What if, instead of trying to force yourself into a strict plan, you embraced the natural ebb and flow of your focus? Welcome to flexible productivity: the art of going with the flow without letting the current sweep you away entirely.

Let's start with an uncomfortable truth: you're not always going to feel productive. Some days you're firing on all cylinders, crossing off tasks left and right, and feeling like a superhero. Other days, just opening an email feels like a Herculean effort. And that's okay. Flexibility means accepting that not every day will be a home run—and giving yourself permission to adapt.

One of the best ways to embrace flexibility is to identify your natural rhythms. Everyone has times of day when they're more focused or energized. Maybe you're a morning person who can tackle big projects before noon, or maybe your brain doesn't really wake up until 3 PM. Instead of fighting against your energy levels, work with them. Schedule your most challenging tasks for when you're naturally at your best and save the low-effort stuff—like replying to emails or organizing files—for your slower hours.

Another key to flexible productivity is the ability to pivot. Sometimes, no matter how much you plan, life throws a wrench into your day. Maybe you had a detailed schedule mapped out, and then your internet went down, or you got stuck on hold with customer service for an hour. Instead of throwing in the towel, adjust. Shift your focus to a different task or use the downtime for a mental break. Productivity isn't about sticking rigidly to a plan—it's about rolling with the punches and finding ways to keep moving forward.

And let's not forget the importance of humor in all of this. Flexibility doesn't just mean adjusting your schedule—it also means adjusting your mindset. When something goes wrong or a task takes twice as long as you expected, laugh about it. Productivity isn't life or death. If you accidentally spend an hour googling "best snacks for procrastinators" instead of working, chalk it up to research and move on.

Part of embracing flexibility is letting go of perfectionism. Not every task needs to be completed perfectly, and not every day needs to be wildly productive. Focus on progress, not perfection. If you only get half your to-do list done, celebrate what you *did* accomplish instead of stressing about what you didn't. A little self-compassion goes a long way in keeping your motivation alive.

One of the greatest advantages of flexible productivity is its ability to work alongside procrastination. By recognizing that procrastination is inevitable, you can build room for it into your day. Allow yourself to take breaks, daydream, or tackle smaller tasks as a way of recharging your mental batteries. This approach prevents procrastination from derailing your entire schedule because you're planning for it rather than pretending it doesn't exist.

But flexibility doesn't mean chaos. It's not about abandoning all structure and doing whatever you feel like at the moment—it's about finding a balance. Use your tools—timers, alarms, and to-do lists— but give yourself permission to adjust them as needed. Productivity isn't a straight line; it's more like a winding road with plenty of detours. The goal is to keep moving, even if the route looks different than you planned.

As you learn to embrace flexibility, you'll find that productivity becomes less of a chore and more of a dance. Some days you'll hit all the right steps, and other days you'll trip over your own feet, but either way, you're still moving forward.

Now that you're comfortable with flexibility, let's introduce one of the simplest and most effective ways to tackle procrastination: committing to just 10 minutes. Even the smallest step can lead to big progress—and we're about to see how.

FIVE

The 10-Minute Rule - Starting Tasks Without Fear

Procrastination thrives on intimidation. Big, scary tasks loom over you like a mountain, and instead of climbing it, you decide to sit at the base, googling "fastest ways to teleport." But what if you didn't have to conquer the whole mountain at once? What if you could start by simply taking one tiny step? Enter the 10-Minute Rule: a genius, procrastinator-friendly method that turns *"I can't do this"* into *"I'll just try for 10 minutes."*

The beauty of this rule is its simplicity. Anyone can commit to just 10 minutes. It's so small, it feels harmless. And yet, it's enough to break through the paralysis of inaction. Once you've started, you might even find yourself sticking with the task longer. The hardest part is always starting—and the 10-Minute Rule is the ultimate trick to outsmart your inner procrastinator. In this chapter, we'll explore how to harness this method to tackle intimidating tasks and build momentum, one tiny effort at a time.

How Committing to Just 10 Minutes Can Overcome Procrastination

The hardest part of any task isn't the doing—it's the starting. That looming project on your to-do list? It's not the actual work that's terrifying; it's the mountain of effort your brain *thinks* it will take. This is where the 10-Minute Rule comes in to save the day. Instead of diving headfirst into a seemingly impossible task, you commit to working on it for just 10 minutes. That's it. Ten measly minutes. It's so small, it feels almost silly to say no—and that's exactly why it works.

Here's the thing about procrastination: it thrives on overwhelm. The larger and scarier a task feels, the more likely you are to avoid it. But the 10-Minute Rule flips the script. By shrinking the task down to a short, manageable time block, it tricks your brain into thinking, *"Well, that's not so bad. I can handle 10 minutes."* You're not committing to the whole mountain—you're just agreeing to take the first step.

The magic of this rule is that it's disarmingly easy. Even on your laziest day, you can probably muster the energy to work for 10 minutes. And because the commitment feels so minor, it removes the mental resistance that keeps you stuck. It's procrastination kryptonite, pure and simple.

Once you start, something surprising often happens: you keep going. It's like that moment when you tell yourself you'll only go to the gym for a quick 10-minute workout, and suddenly you're sweating through a full 30-minute session. (Okay, maybe not *suddenly*, but you get the idea.) Starting creates momentum, and momentum carries you forward. Before you know it, those 10 minutes stretch into 20 or 30, and you've accomplished more than you thought possible.

But here's the catch: you don't *have* to keep going. The brilliance of the 10-Minute Rule is that it works whether you do more or not. If you hit your 10 minutes and decide you're done, that's still a win. You've made progress, no matter how small, and that's better than doing nothing at all. It's the perfect balance of low pressure and high reward.

Let's say you're avoiding a task that feels overwhelming, like writing a report. Instead of staring at a blank screen and spiraling into despair, set a timer for 10 minutes and tell yourself, *"I'll just write the first sentence."* That's it. Nothing fancy, no grand expectations—just one sentence. Odds are, once you've written that sentence, the rest won't seem so daunting. But even if it does, you've still made a dent. And that dent is the start of real progress.

The 10-Minute Rule also works wonders for chores and errands. Need to clean your kitchen but can't face the mountain of dishes? Set a timer for 10 minutes and see how much you can get done. Even if you don't finish, you've chipped away at the task, and the mountain is now a smaller hill. Plus, there's something oddly satisfying about racing the clock—procrastination, but make it sporty.

This rule isn't just about tasks you hate, either. It's a great way to start projects you're excited about but feel too intimidated to begin. Have you been daydreaming about writing a book or learning to paint? Commit to 10 minutes a day. The low stakes make it easy to start, and those short sessions add up over time. You might just find that your procrastination melts away when the task feels achievable.

The best part? The 10-Minute Rule isn't about perfection. It's not about doing everything or even doing it well—it's about starting. Progress, no matter how small, is still progress. And once you've proven to yourself that you can handle 10 minutes, you'll start to believe you can handle more.

So, the next time you're stuck in procrastination limbo, give the 10-Minute Rule a try. Set a timer, take a deep breath, and dive in. You might surprise yourself with how far those 10 minutes can take you.

Practical Advice for Breaking Down Intimidating Tasks

Big, intimidating tasks have a way of paralyzing even the most ambitious among us. You stare at your to-do list, and there it is, taunting you: "Finish the 20-page report," "Plan the entire office holiday party," or "Finally fix the leaking sink." It's no wonder you find yourself reaching for distractions like alphabetizing your bookshelf or Googling "how to move to a tiny house in the woods." The problem isn't the task itself—it's the sheer size of it. The solution? Break it down into smaller, manageable pieces.

Think about it this way: eating a whole pizza in one bite is impossible (and frankly, dangerous), but eating it slice by slice? Totally doable. The same applies to your overwhelming task. Instead of focusing on the entire thing, identify the tiniest step you can take to get started. If you're writing a report, that step might be as simple as opening a blank document. Not typing anything—just opening it. Does it feel like progress? Barely. But here's the magic: once you've started, you've already defeated the hardest part—beginning.

When a task feels insurmountable, breaking it into bite-sized chunks makes it approachable. Writing a 20-page report sounds terrifying, but brainstorming three bullet points for the introduction? Not so bad. After you have those three bullet points, maybe you'll feel ready to flesh out one of them into a paragraph. Before you know it, you're building momentum, and the task that once felt impossible is well underway.

This approach works for any daunting chore. If your goal is to clean the entire garage, start with one corner. If you're planning an event, focus on booking the venue first. Completing just one small piece of the puzzle gives you a sense of progress and reduces the overwhelming weight of the larger goal. It's procrastination's worst enemy: small, consistent action.

But here's the secret weapon to really overcoming the intimidation: limit your commitment. Promise yourself that you'll work on the task for just five or ten minutes. This removes the pressure of feeling like you need to finish the whole thing. You're not agreeing to scale the mountain—you're just committing to tying your boots. And the best part? Once you start, you'll often find yourself naturally wanting to continue. Momentum is a powerful thing, but it only works if you take that first step.

Visualization can also work wonders. Sometimes, tasks feel overwhelming because they exist in a fog of undefined steps. Clearing that fog can help you see the path forward. Take a piece of paper and map out the smaller tasks involved. For example, if your goal is to "plan the office holiday party," jot down every little thing you need to do: choose a date, book the venue, send invitations, pick a playlist. Suddenly, it's not one massive task—it's a series of manageable steps. Each one feels less like a mountain and more like a stepping stone.

Celebrating your progress is equally important. Did you complete a small task? Great! Give yourself a high-five, a cookie, or five minutes of guilt-free relaxation. These mini-rewards reinforce the behavior of taking action and make the process feel less like a grind. When you're tackling a big project, those small victories are the fuel that keeps you moving forward.

It's also worth reminding yourself that perfection is not the goal. One of procrastination's sneakiest tricks is convincing you that if you can't do something perfectly, you shouldn't do it at all. Fight back by giving yourself permission to do it badly. Write a messy first draft, sort the garage haphazardly, or pick a venue that's "good enough." Progress is better than perfection because it gets you closer to the finish line.

The key to breaking down intimidating tasks is to make them feel achievable. When you stop seeing the whole mountain and focus on just the first step, the fear starts to melt away. Start small, celebrate every step, and remind yourself that progress—even in tiny doses—is still progress. Once you've tackled one piece, you'll be ready for the next. The mountain may still be there, but with each small step, it becomes less of a threat and more of an adventure.

How Small Starts Lead to Productive Momentum

Procrastination thrives on convincing you that starting is the hardest part. It says things like, *"This will take forever,"* or, *"You need to have all the details perfectly lined up before you can begin."* The result? You freeze, avoiding the task entirely. But here's the secret procrastination doesn't want you to know: all it takes to break that paralysis is one small action. A tiny, laughably simple start can create the momentum you need to turn avoidance into achievement.

Momentum works like a snowball rolling downhill. It starts with something small—a clump of snow—and as it rolls, it builds speed and size, becoming unstoppable. Your productivity works the same way. The tiniest action—writing a single sentence, moving one item off your desk, or setting up a document—can set off a chain reaction. Once you're in motion, the task becomes easier, and suddenly, you're doing the very thing you've been avoiding.

The trick is to set the bar for starting so low that it feels impossible to fail. If you're procrastinating on writing a report, don't think about finishing the entire thing. Instead, commit to opening a blank document and typing one word. Yes, just one. It might seem absurdly small, but that's the point—it's so easy that even your most stubborn inner procrastinator can't argue with it. And once that first word is written, the next comes more naturally. Before you know it, you've written a sentence, then a paragraph, and momentum is doing the heavy lifting.

This approach works because small actions generate energy. When you're idle, the task feels heavier than it actually is. But when you take even the tiniest step, your brain shifts gears. You move from thinking *"I can't do this"* to *"What's next?"* That shift creates momentum, and suddenly the task feels less like an overwhelming mountain and more like a series of manageable steps.

Momentum thrives on quick wins. Each small task you complete—no matter how minor—sends a message to your brain: *"Progress is happening!"* This is why things like making your bed or organizing your desk can set the tone for a productive day. They're small victories that give you a sense of accomplishment, fueling your motivation to tackle the next step.

To build momentum, focus on what's easy. Start with something so small it feels almost silly. Need to clean your room? Start by throwing one piece of trash into the bin. Have a massive report to write? Begin by jotting down a title. These small starts don't feel like work, but they create movement—and movement is everything. Once you've started, it's much harder to stop.

Starting small also means giving yourself permission to be messy. Perfectionism is procrastination's best friend. If you feel like the first draft has to be flawless, you're more likely to avoid starting altogether. Instead, aim to create something imperfect. A messy first draft is still progress. Sorting papers into rough piles is better than letting them scatter. The goal isn't perfection—it's movement. You can always refine things later, but you can't edit or organize something that doesn't exist.

Momentum isn't just about starting—it also makes it easier to return to a task. Once you've begun, the project becomes less intimidating because you've already made progress. Even if you only worked for five or ten minutes, the familiarity of having started makes picking it back up feel less daunting. It's like saying to yourself, *"Hey, I've already done part of this, so I can definitely keep going."*

And don't forget to celebrate small starts. Each time you take that initial step, you're proving to yourself that you can overcome procrastination. Finished one sentence? Applaud yourself. Cleared one section of your desk? Take a victory lap around the house. Small wins build confidence, which makes starting even easier the next time.

Procrastination loves to make tasks seem overwhelming, but small starts expose that bluff. By focusing on one tiny action, you turn dread into progress and hesitation into momentum. The next time you feel stuck, don't focus on the mountain. Just take the first step. One small start leads to another, and before you know it, you're halfway there.

Tips for "Tricking" Yourself Into Action Through Mini-Goals

Procrastination loves to make every task feel like an insurmountable mountain. That's where mini-goals come in: small, manageable objectives that shrink the mountain into a series of tiny hills. By focusing on one small step at a time, you trick your brain into action without overwhelming it. Suddenly, the task that felt impossible seems like something you can actually tackle.

Mini-goals work because they make starting easier. Instead of looking at a massive to-do like *"Write a report,"* you break it down into something ridiculously small, like *"Write the title"* or *"Jot down one idea."* These micro-tasks feel so doable, your brain can't argue with them. Once you've completed one step, the momentum builds, and taking the next step becomes easier.

For instance, imagine you've been putting off cleaning your garage. The thought of tackling it all is exhausting, so instead, you decide to set a mini-goal: organize one shelf. Just one. It's not intimidating, and once you've started, you'll likely find yourself moving on to the next shelf without much resistance. That's the power of mini-goals—

they get you moving, and movement is the antidote to procrastination.

A clever way to use mini-goals is to focus on time instead of the result. Instead of saying, *"I'll finish my presentation,"* tell yourself, *"I'll work on it for 10 minutes."* This approach makes the task feel less like a monumental commitment. Once the timer starts, you're likely to keep going beyond the 10 minutes because starting is the hardest part. Even if you stop at 10 minutes, you've still made progress, and that's a win.

Pairing mini-goals with rewards makes them even more effective. Promise yourself a cup of coffee after writing one paragraph or a short video break after completing five emails. The reward creates positive reinforcement, making the task feel less like a chore and more like an opportunity to earn a treat. Just make sure the reward doesn't derail your progress—finishing one sentence doesn't earn you an hour-long Netflix binge.

Mini-goals also transform tedious tasks. If you're procrastinating on something boring, like data entry, set a goal to input information for just 10 rows. That's it. By breaking the task into small, digestible pieces, you make it bearable. Each completed mini-goal gives you a sense of accomplishment, keeping your motivation alive.

The key is specificity. Vague goals like *"make progress on the project"* don't work because they lack clarity. Instead, choose something concrete: *"Draft the introduction"* or *"Organize three files."* This focus helps you stay on track and measure your progress. And with each small step, the mountain shrinks until it's no longer intimidating.

Mini-goals are also excellent for starting creative projects. Want to write a novel but can't face a blank page? Set a goal to write 50 words. Just 50. It feels too small to fail, but once you've started, you might find yourself writing 500. Creativity flows more freely when you remove the pressure to deliver something perfect.

The beauty of mini-goals is their adaptability. On low-energy days, your goal might be as small as *"open the document."* On productive days, you can scale up to *"write two paragraphs."* By tailoring your mini-goals to your capacity, you stay productive without burning out.

By breaking tasks into mini-goals, you trick procrastination into submission. No longer is the task an overwhelming monster; it's a manageable series of steps. Each small action leads to the next, and before you know it, you've made significant progress.

And while mini-goals are great for getting started, what happens when you're naturally distracted? Instead of fighting those distractions, you can learn to use them as part of your productivity strategy. Let's dive into how channeling distractions can actually boost your focus and energy.

SIX

"Distraction-Switching" to Stay Energized

Distractions get a bad rap. They're often painted as productivity's mortal enemy, the little devils pulling your attention away from your noble pursuit of getting things done. But what if distractions weren't the villains of your workday? What if, instead of fighting them, you embraced them—and even made them work for you? Welcome to the world of "distraction-switching," where the art of juggling multiple diversions becomes your secret weapon for staying energized and focused.

This chapter isn't about eliminating distractions (good luck with that). It's about learning how to channel them into productive breaks and clever pivots that keep your brain engaged. Because let's be honest—sometimes the best way to focus on one task is to step away from it altogether, even if that means folding laundry, reorganizing your pantry, or watching a video about how octopuses dream. In this chapter, we'll explore how to harness the power of distractions and use them to recharge your brain without losing sight of your goals.

Channeling Natural Distractions Into Productive Short Breaks

Distractions are like uninvited guests at the productivity party. They show up unannounced, demand your attention, and before you know it, you're Googling "how to make artisan pickles" instead of tackling your to-do list. But here's the thing: distractions don't have to ruin your day. In fact, they can be the perfect excuse for a productive short break—if you know how to use them.

Let's start by redefining distractions. Instead of seeing them as interruptions, think of them as opportunities for a mental reset. Your brain isn't built to stay hyper-focused for hours on end. It needs breaks to recharge, and distractions are its way of saying, *"Hey, let's take a breather before we crash."* The key is to turn those distractions into intentional pauses that benefit your workflow rather than derailing it entirely.

For example, imagine you're working on a report when you feel the urge to scroll social media. Instead of mindlessly diving into your favorite app, use that moment to step away and do something physically engaging. Take a walk, stretch, or tidy up your workspace. These activities still count as distractions, but they're active ones that give your brain the reset it needs without draining your energy. Bonus: you've accomplished something useful, which feels a lot better than realizing you just spent 20 minutes watching someone lip-sync to '90s pop hits.

Another way to channel distractions is to lean into them—but with boundaries. Say you're suddenly fascinated by an article on "why flamingos are pink." Set a timer for five or ten minutes to indulge your curiosity guilt-free, then return to your task. By giving yourself permission to explore a distraction, you satisfy your brain's craving for novelty while keeping the interruption from spiraling out of control. It's procrastination with a leash.

Distractions can also double as mini-rewards. If you've been focused for a solid block of time, let yourself engage in something fun or silly as a treat. Just finished drafting a tricky email? Take five minutes to check out that viral video everyone's talking about. These short, intentional breaks keep you motivated without letting distractions take over your day. It's like saying to your brain, *"Good job, here's a snack—now back to work."*

Physical distractions are another great tool for productive breaks. When your focus starts to wane, get up and move. Water your plants, fold a load of laundry, or do a quick round of jumping jacks (if you're feeling ambitious). These activities wake up your body and give your mind a chance to wander, which often leads to surprising bursts of creativity. Some of your best ideas might strike while you're vacuuming or organizing your sock drawer—it's just how the brain works.

The beauty of distraction-switching is that it helps you maintain your energy throughout the day. Instead of burning out by forcing yourself to stay laser-focused for hours, you alternate between work and engaging breaks. This rhythm not only keeps your brain fresh but also makes it easier to dive back into your tasks when the break is over. It's a win-win.

Of course, not all distractions are created equal. The key is to choose ones that re-energize you rather than drain you. Passive distractions, like binge-watching TV or endlessly scrolling, tend to sap your energy, leaving you feeling sluggish and guilty. Active distractions, on the other hand, involve movement, creativity, or curiosity. They engage your brain in a different way, giving it the recharge it needs to return to work with renewed focus.

Remember, the goal isn't to eliminate distractions altogether—it's to manage them in a way that supports your productivity. By reframing distractions as short, intentional breaks, you can turn them from obstacles into tools. So the next time your mind starts to wander, don't panic. Take a pause, embrace the distraction, and use it to your advantage. Your brain will thank you.

And as you get better at using distractions to your benefit, you'll discover that switching between tasks can also be a surprisingly effective way to stay energized and avoid burnout. Let's explore how multitasking with intention can keep you moving forward.

The Benefits of Task-Switching for Re-Energizing Your Brain

We've all been there: you're slogging through a task, and suddenly your brain feels like it's wading through quicksand. Concentration dwindles, frustration builds, and the thought of continuing feels unbearable. Enter task-switching—a productivity hack that feels counterintuitive but works wonders. By momentarily shifting gears and focusing on a different task, you can re-energize your brain and return to your original work with fresh focus and vigor.

The logic behind task-switching is simple. Your brain thrives on variety. When you spend too much time on one activity, your mental energy starts to deplete, making even the simplest tasks feel overwhelming. Switching to a different type of task—preferably one that engages a different part of your brain—gives your mind a much-needed break without completely stepping away from productivity.

Let's say you're knee-deep in a project requiring intense concentration, like analyzing data or writing a report. Instead of forcing yourself to power through when your focus starts to wane, switch to a lower-pressure task, like organizing your workspace or replying to emails. These activities use different mental muscles, allowing the overworked part of your brain to recover while still getting things done. It's like giving your brain a quick workout on the elliptical after sprinting on a treadmill.

Task-switching is particularly effective for procrastinators because it transforms avoidance into action. Imagine you've been avoiding a dreaded project all morning. Instead of fighting that resistance, embrace it—but on your terms. Switch to a smaller, less intimidating task, like drafting a quick email or brainstorming ideas for a different project. Completing even one small thing shifts your mindset from *"I can't do anything"* to *"Hey, I'm getting things done."* That confidence boost often makes it easier to circle back to the original task.

But task-switching isn't about chaotic multitasking. Jumping between too many tasks at random can scatter your focus and leave you feeling even more overwhelmed. The key is to switch intentionally. Choose tasks that complement each other, like pairing a creative activity with an administrative one, or alternating between physically active and sedentary work. This balance prevents burnout while keeping you engaged.

One of the best ways to make task-switching work is to use time limits. Instead of abandoning one task entirely, set a timer for 15 or 20 minutes to work on something different. This creates a clear boundary, so you don't accidentally spend the entire afternoon reorganizing your closet when you're supposed to be finishing a proposal. When the timer goes off, you can decide whether to return to the original task or continue with the new one. Either way, you've made progress.

Switching between tasks also helps spark creativity. Ever notice how your best ideas seem to pop up when you're doing something completely unrelated to the problem you're trying to solve? That's because your brain makes connections more easily when it's not hyper-focused on one thing. By stepping away from a challenging task and working on something different, you give your mind the space to think more freely. Suddenly, the solution you couldn't see before becomes obvious.

For example, if you're stuck on a creative project, switch to something more methodical, like organizing your files or writing a list. Conversely, if you're bogged down by administrative work, switch to a creative task, like sketching out ideas or drafting a rough plan. This change in focus recharges your brain while keeping your productivity flowing.

Task-switching isn't just about productivity—it's also about energy management. It acknowledges that your brain isn't a machine that can grind endlessly on one task. By respecting your mental limits and giving yourself permission to shift gears, you can maintain a steady, sustainable level of focus throughout the day.

The next time you feel stuck or drained, don't push through the exhaustion. Instead, switch gears. Move to a different task, set a timer, and let your brain enjoy the variety. You'll be amazed at how much easier it is to return to your original work with a clear head and renewed energy.

And while task-switching is great for maintaining focus, it's equally important to embrace the distractions and daydreams that come with it. Let's explore how productive daydreaming can transform idle moments into creative breakthroughs.

Using Distractions Mindfully to Avoid Burnout and Boredom

Distractions often feel like the enemy of productivity, but they don't have to be. When used mindfully, they can be the secret weapon that keeps you from spiraling into burnout or drowning in boredom. The trick isn't to eliminate distractions completely (impossible), but to harness them as intentional pauses that re-energize your brain and keep your day moving forward.

First, let's acknowledge the reality: long, repetitive tasks can drain your mental energy. Boredom sets in, and suddenly you're daydreaming about how to become a professional jetpack tester. This is when a distraction can actually be helpful. Instead of fighting the urge, plan for it. Build short, intentional distraction breaks into your routine. For every 25–30 minutes of focused work, give yourself five minutes to indulge in something light and fun—whether it's scrolling through memes, checking social media, or watching a quick video of baby goats in pajamas. The key is to set a timer so you don't slip into a full-blown procrastination binge.

These breaks act as mental resets. They give your brain a chance to recover from intense focus and make it easier to return to your task feeling refreshed. Think of them as palate cleansers for your mind. Instead of feeling guilty for being distracted, you'll feel recharged and ready to dive back in.

Distractions can also be used to combat burnout. High-pressure tasks and endless to-do lists can leave even the most diligent worker feeling frazzled. A light-hearted distraction—like playing a quick puzzle game or watching a funny clip—can help you decompress. Humor and joy are powerful burnout busters, and giving yourself permission to laugh or unwind for a few minutes can make all the difference in how you approach the rest of your day.

Physical distractions are another great way to reset. When your focus starts to fade, step away from your desk and do something active. Take a walk, stretch, or do a quick household chore. Movement engages a different part of your brain, giving the overworked part a chance to rest. Plus, many people find their best ideas come when they're not actively thinking about a problem—like while folding laundry or watering plants.

If your distractions tend to be more creative, lean into them. Doodling, brainstorming, or working on a side project can be a form of productive procrastination. You're still engaging your mind, but without the pressure of sticking to your main task. These activities can spark ideas that feed back into your primary work, giving you a creative boost while still feeling like a break.

The key to using distractions wisely is awareness. Pay attention to why you're distracted. Are you genuinely tired and in need of a reset, or are you avoiding something that feels overwhelming? If it's the latter, try pairing your distraction with a tiny step toward your goal. For example, if you're procrastinating on a report, allow yourself to sip coffee or doodle while jotting down a few bullet points. Combining a distraction with a small action lets you satisfy your need for a break while still making progress.

Not all distractions are created equal. Passive distractions, like mindlessly scrolling through social media or binge-watching videos, often drain your energy and leave you feeling guilty. Active distractions, like taking a walk, doing a quick chore, or reading something interesting, tend to refresh your brain and provide more value. Choose wisely—your future self will thank you.

The most important thing to remember is that distractions aren't inherently bad. They're a natural part of how your brain works, and when used intentionally, they can improve your focus and productivity. By reframing distractions as tools rather than obstacles, you can integrate them into your day in a way that keeps you energized and motivated.

And while intentional breaks are helpful, there's another kind of wandering that can be even more powerful: daydreaming. Far from being a waste of time, letting your mind wander can spark creativity and lead to unexpected breakthroughs. Let's explore how to embrace productive daydreaming and use it to your advantage.

Humor About Embracing Distractions as Part of the Process

Distractions are the Houdinis of productivity. One minute, you're laser-focused, and the next, you're watching a tutorial on how to build a treehouse—despite not having kids, trees, or any desire to own power tools. But what if we stopped fighting distractions and started laughing at their inevitability? By embracing them as part of the process, you can turn these interruptions into productivity's quirky sidekick, rather than its archnemesis.

The first step to embracing distractions is to admit they're unavoidable. You're not a productivity robot (if you are, please update your software). No matter how disciplined you think you are, your brain is going to wander. The email you're drafting will somehow lead to you Googling "how long can cats hold grudges," and before you know it, you've learned more about feline psychology than anyone asked for. Instead of beating yourself up about these detours, acknowledge them as a natural part of how your mind works.

In fact, distractions can even be helpful—when handled correctly. Ever notice how stepping away from a task for a few minutes often leads to a breakthrough? That's because your brain does some of its best problem-solving when you're not forcing it to focus. Think of distractions as the mental equivalent of stretching during a long run. Sure, they slow you down temporarily, but they also prevent you from burning out.

One of the funniest things about distractions is how creative they can be. When faced with a task you don't want to do, your brain becomes a master escape artist, conjuring up urgent "priorities" like alphabetizing your spices or reorganizing your sock drawer. These moments are worth laughing at—because honestly, isn't it hilarious how quickly you'll abandon something important to untangle old headphones?

The trick to making distractions work for you is to lean into them without letting them take over. Give yourself permission to embrace a distraction briefly, then channel it into something productive. For example, if you're scrolling through your favorite memes, use that time to gather inspiration for a project. Or if you're deep-cleaning your desk to avoid starting a report, enjoy the tidying spree—but set a timer so you don't end up Marie Kondo-ing your entire house.

Humor also plays a crucial role in dealing with distractions. Instead of getting frustrated when you realize you've spent 20 minutes learning about octopus intelligence, laugh it off. Productivity isn't a straight line; it's more like a roller coaster with random detours into funhouse mirrors. By keeping a sense of humor about your distractions, you'll stop seeing them as failures and start seeing them as part of the journey.

Distractions can also make your workday more enjoyable—when you control them. Build intentional distractions into your schedule as little "productivity palate cleansers." After 30 minutes of focused work, give yourself five minutes to explore whatever weird curiosity has been tugging at your brain. These planned interruptions act as rewards, keeping you motivated and preventing the guilt spiral of accidental procrastination.

But the best part of embracing distractions is how they can lead to unexpected creativity. Some of the world's greatest ideas have come from minds wandering off the beaten path. That silly cat video might spark an idea for your next project. That random article about Icelandic hot springs might lead to the perfect metaphor for your pitch. By letting your brain play, you give it room to make connections you wouldn't find if you were forcing yourself to focus.

In the end, distractions aren't productivity's enemy—they're just a little unruly. When you laugh at their absurdity, manage them with humor, and use them to recharge, they can become an unlikely ally in your quest to get things done. The key is balance: let them exist without letting them take over.

Now that you've learned how to embrace and even enjoy distractions, it's time to explore the kind of mental wandering that goes beyond mere interruptions. Daydreaming, when done right, can be a powerful tool for creativity and problem-solving. In the next chapter, we'll discover how you can turn idle thoughts into productive breakthroughs.

SEVEN

Productive Daydreaming and the Power of Imagination

Daydreaming often gets a bad reputation as the antithesis of productivity. It's what you do when you're bored, zoning out, or trying to escape reality by imagining yourself as the star of an action movie where you save the world with a perfectly timed, witty comeback. But what if daydreaming wasn't a waste of time? What if, instead, it was one of the most powerful tools for creativity, problem-solving, and even productivity?

In this chapter, we'll explore how letting your mind wander can actually help you tackle challenges and generate ideas in ways focused thinking can't. By learning to harness the natural drift of your imagination, you can transform idle moments into valuable opportunities for insight and innovation. Daydreaming isn't about avoiding work—it's about unlocking your brain's full potential, one meandering thought at a time.

How to Harness Creative Daydreaming for Brainstorming and Insights

Daydreaming is often dismissed as wasted time, but it's one of the brain's most powerful tools for brainstorming and gaining insights. When your mind wanders, it enters a state called the **default mode network** (DMN)—a resting state where ideas flow freely, unburdened by logic or focus. This is why your best ideas often hit you while you're showering, walking, or doing something completely unrelated to work. Daydreaming, far from being a distraction, is actually your brain solving problems in the background.

To use daydreaming productively, you need to create the right conditions. Start by stepping away from tasks that demand intense focus. Instead, engage in low-effort activities like walking, gardening, or washing dishes. These actions keep your body occupied while leaving your mind free to roam. The rhythmic nature of these tasks— steps on a trail or the gentle scrubbing of a plate—encourages the DMN to kick in, letting ideas bubble to the surface.

Take walking, for example. Studies show that walking, especially outdoors, boosts creativity. The combination of light movement and a change of scenery stimulates your brain's idea factory. Many great thinkers, like Charles Darwin and Steve Jobs, swore by their walking routines for this very reason. When you let your mind wander, it often stumbles onto connections or solutions you couldn't find by staring at a screen.

To steer your daydreaming in a productive direction, plant a seed before you step away. Think briefly about the challenge or project you're tackling. Then, let go and engage in your chosen activity. While you're folding laundry or strolling through the park, your brain will keep working on the problem behind the scenes. This is mental outsourcing at its finest—your subconscious tackles the hard work while you take a break.

Having a way to capture ideas as they emerge is also essential. Keep a notebook or voice memo app handy to jot down thoughts before they slip away. Sometimes, a stray idea that seems unrelated can unlock the solution to your main problem. Whether it's a metaphor, a new approach, or a sudden realization, these insights are the gems of productive daydreaming. Recording them ensures they don't vanish into the ether.

Music can also enhance daydreaming. Instrumental or ambient tracks without lyrics are especially helpful. Choose music that matches the mood of your task. If you need a spark of energy, pick something upbeat. For deeper thinking, go with something calming or atmospheric. Music helps set the tone for your mind's creative wanderings without pulling focus away from the task at hand.

One surprising benefit of daydreaming is its ability to provide a broader perspective. When you're laser-focused on a project, it's easy to get bogged down in details. Daydreaming pulls you back, offering a bird's-eye view of the problem. From this wider angle, patterns, solutions, and connections often become clearer. It's like stepping away from a puzzle to see how all the pieces fit together.

But as with anything, balance is key. Unstructured daydreaming can turn into unproductive daydreaming if you're not careful. Set boundaries for your wandering mind. For example, allow yourself 10–15 minutes to drift, then check in to see if anything useful has surfaced. If not, no worries—you've still given your brain the rest it needs. If something valuable does emerge, capture it immediately and build on it while it's fresh.

The beauty of daydreaming is its accessibility. You don't need special tools, expensive apps, or fancy techniques. You simply need to give yourself permission to let your mind wander. When approached intentionally, daydreaming becomes a powerful form of brainstorming—one that taps into creativity and problem-solving in ways structured thinking can't.

So, the next time you're stuck, step away, do something mundane, and let your mind drift. You might be surprised at what your brain discovers when it's free to roam. Daydreaming isn't time wasted; it's imagination unleashed.

Using Visualization as a Powerful, Non-Action-Oriented Tool

Visualization is daydreaming's more structured and ambitious cousin —the one who shows up with a vision board and a five-year plan. While daydreaming lets your mind wander freely, visualization gives it a direction, making it a powerful tool for creativity, problem-solving, and goal-setting. The beauty of visualization is that it doesn't require immediate action. Instead, it helps you mentally rehearse success, paving the way for real-world results.

At its core, visualization is about creating mental pictures of what you want to achieve. Athletes use it all the time to enhance performance. They imagine themselves running the perfect race, sinking the perfect shot, or nailing their routine. It's not just fluff— science backs it up. Studies show that mentally rehearsing actions activates the same neural pathways as physically performing them. So, even if you're not moving a muscle, your brain is practicing, priming you for success when it's go-time.

You don't have to be an Olympic athlete to benefit from visualization. Imagine you're preparing for a big presentation. Instead of diving straight into your slides, spend a few minutes visualizing how you want it to go. Picture yourself standing confidently, delivering your key points with ease, and fielding questions like a pro. This mental rehearsal doesn't just build confidence—it also reduces anxiety by making the scenario feel more familiar. Your brain, in its infinite wisdom, thinks, *"Oh, we've done this before,"* even though you haven't.

Visualization is also a fantastic tool for problem-solving. Let's say you're stuck on a tricky project. Instead of beating your head against the wall, take a step back and visualize the outcome you want. What does the finished project look like? How do all the pieces fit together? By focusing on the end result, you can often work backward to figure out the next steps. It's like reverse-engineering your way to a solution.

One of the most enjoyable aspects of visualization is how creative you can get with it. You're not bound by reality here—dream big. Want to write a best-selling novel? Picture yourself at a book signing, a long line of adoring fans waiting to meet you. Trying to ace a test? Visualize breezing through each question with confidence. The goal isn't to make these scenarios your sole focus but to use them as motivation. When you can see your success clearly, it becomes easier to work toward it.

To make visualization more effective, engage all your senses. Don't just see yourself giving that presentation—hear the applause, feel the clicker in your hand, and sense the calm confidence radiating through you. The more vivid the image, the more real it feels to your brain. This sensory-rich experience cements the vision in your mind, making it a powerful motivator when it's time to act.

If you struggle with staying focused while visualizing, try pairing it with mindfulness techniques. Start with a few deep breaths to clear your mind, then guide yourself through the scenario step by step. This approach helps keep your thoughts on track and prevents your brain from veering off into *"what's for dinner?"* territory.

But visualization isn't just about outcomes—it's also useful for the process. If you're tackling a big project, visualize yourself working on it efficiently and staying in the zone. Picture the steps you'll take, the tools you'll use, and the mini-milestones you'll hit along the way. This not only makes the task feel less daunting but also gives you a mental roadmap to follow.

Of course, visualization isn't a magic wand. You still have to do the work. But by mentally rehearsing success, you set the stage for a smoother, more confident execution. Think of it as pre-loading your brain with the instructions it needs to get the job done.

The power of visualization lies in its simplicity. You don't need special tools or extra time—just your imagination and a willingness to dream. When combined with action, it can turn your wildest ideas into achievable goals. So, the next time you're stuck or intimidated by what lies ahead, close your eyes, take a deep breath, and picture your success. Sometimes, seeing is the first step to believing—and achieving.

Setting Boundaries on Daydreaming Time for Balanced Productivity

Daydreaming is a powerful tool, but without boundaries, it can derail even the best-laid plans. What starts as a creative brainstorming session can quickly turn into imagining yourself as a world-famous salsa dancer, far removed from the task at hand. The key to using daydreaming productively is to set limits, ensuring it sparks creativity without consuming your entire day.

The first step is recognizing when you're daydreaming. Often, it sneaks up on you: one minute, you're working, and the next, you're mentally designing the perfect treehouse. Take note of when your mind begins to wander and why. Are you procrastinating on a difficult task, or is your brain naturally seeking a break? Knowing the difference helps you decide whether to rein it in or embrace it.

Once you've identified the daydreaming urge, set time limits. Structure your day with dedicated "daydreaming sessions" of 10–15 minutes. Use a timer to prevent these breaks from stretching into hours. Knowing there's a hard stop encourages you to enjoy the moment without guilt and keeps your day on track. Think of it as letting your imagination take a short recess—just enough time to wander before returning to focus.

Pairing daydreaming with physical activities can also help keep it productive. Walking, stretching, or light chores are great companions to mental wandering. These activities act as natural time constraints: when the walk ends or the dishwasher is loaded, your daydreaming session is over. Plus, physical movement stimulates your brain, making your ideas sharper and more creative.

It's important to distinguish between productive and unproductive daydreaming. Productive daydreaming has a loose focus. You might brainstorm ideas, visualize a solution, or imagine future success. Unproductive daydreaming, however, tends to wander aimlessly into unrelated or overly indulgent territory, like replaying awkward moments from years ago or planning hypothetical arguments you'll never have. While harmless in small doses, too much of this kind of daydreaming can sap your energy and leave you feeling scattered.

To keep your daydreaming on track, "plant a seed" before letting your mind wander. Briefly focus on the challenge or goal you're working on, then step away and let your imagination take over. For example, if you're stuck on a work problem, think about it for a moment, then take a walk. Your brain will often keep processing the problem subconsciously, leading to surprising insights when you return.

For those prone to getting lost in daydreaming, having a clear "pause point" can help. Tell yourself, *"I'll let my mind wander while I fold laundry, but when I'm done, I'll spend 15 minutes writing that report."* Creating a concrete plan ensures that your daydreaming session ends with a smooth transition back to productivity.

If you find yourself consistently daydreaming at inconvenient times, consider scheduling it at the beginning or end of your day. Morning daydreaming can inspire creative thinking and set a positive tone for the hours ahead, while evening sessions can help you unwind and process the day. By dedicating specific times to daydreaming, you free yourself from the guilt of zoning out when you're supposed to be working.

Boundaries also mean recognizing when daydreaming isn't serving you. If you notice your thoughts spiraling into unproductive or stressful territory—like rehashing past failures—it's time to redirect your attention. Use grounding techniques like taking deep breaths, making a quick list, or engaging in a focused physical task to bring your mind back to the present.

The beauty of setting limits on daydreaming is that it doesn't stifle your creativity—it amplifies it. By allowing your mind to wander within structured boundaries, you gain the benefits of imagination without letting it derail your goals. It's a balance of freedom and focus, ensuring that your daydreams remain a source of inspiration rather than a distraction.

Now that you've learned to guide your wandering thoughts, it's time to connect them to real goals. Let's explore specific exercises that help turn those imaginative daydreams into practical, actionable ideas.

Fun Exercises to Keep Daydreams Connected to Real Goals

Daydreams are like butterflies—beautiful, fleeting, and often impossible to catch. But what if you could corral those imaginative flutters into something useful? By practicing a few targeted exercises, you can channel your daydreams into creative breakthroughs and connect them to real, actionable goals. The key is to treat your imagination like a brainstorming partner rather than a rogue force pulling you away from your plans.

One of the simplest ways to guide your daydreaming is to ask yourself an open-ended question before letting your mind wander. For example: *"What's the best way to solve this problem?"* or *"What's a bold, unconventional idea I haven't considered yet?"* These prompts act as gentle anchors, steering your thoughts toward productive territory. It's not about forcing a solution—just planting a seed and letting your subconscious do the work.

Another great exercise is **"what-if" scenarios.** This playful approach involves imagining the wildest possibilities, no matter how impractical they seem. For example, if you're struggling with a work project, ask yourself, *"What if I had unlimited resources?"* or *"What if I started over entirely?"* By exploring these extreme scenarios, you give yourself permission to think outside the box, often uncovering ideas you wouldn't have considered otherwise.

Visualization exercises can also help tether daydreams to goals. Instead of letting your thoughts wander aimlessly, guide them with a clear outcome in mind. Picture your goal in vivid detail—what it looks like, feels like, and sounds like when it's achieved. If you're preparing for a big presentation, imagine yourself delivering it confidently, hearing applause, and answering questions with ease. The more vivid your visualization, the more real it feels, which motivates you to make it happen.

Mind-mapping is another effective tool for turning daydreams into tangible ideas. Start with a central idea or problem, and let your imagination branch out in all directions. As your thoughts meander, jot down connections, solutions, and creative insights. Mind-mapping mimics the natural flow of daydreaming but captures its results in a way that's easy to revisit later. Plus, it's a great excuse to use colorful pens and feel like a creative genius.

For those who find their daydreams spiraling into unrelated territory (we've all planned our Academy Award speeches mid-project), a journaling exercise can help refocus. Set a timer for five minutes and write down every thought that comes to mind, no matter how random. Once the timer goes off, scan your notes for any ideas that might apply to your current goals. Even seemingly unrelated musings can spark connections when viewed in a different context.

If you're a fan of collaboration, consider turning your daydreaming into a shared activity. Brainstorming with a friend or colleague can turn your wandering thoughts into a productive conversation. Share your wildest ideas and encourage them to do the same. This process not only generates new insights but also keeps you accountable—you're less likely to drift into unrelated tangents when someone else is in the room.

Finally, don't forget to celebrate the process itself. Daydreaming isn't just a means to an end; it's a way of engaging with your creativity and imagination. Whether your wandering thoughts lead to a breakthrough or simply provide a refreshing mental break, they're a valuable part of your workflow. Laugh at the silly tangents, embrace the surprising insights, and give yourself credit for letting your mind roam.

Daydreaming is a skill that, when honed, can transform idle thoughts into powerful tools for progress. By practicing these exercises, you'll not only keep your imagination tethered to real-world goals but also unlock new levels of creativity and problem-solving. The more you practice, the more naturally your daydreams will align with your ambitions.

As your daydreaming evolves into a tool for action, it's worth considering another skill that every great procrastinator should master: the fine art of looking busy. After all, appearances matter—and knowing how to seem productive can buy you the time you need to make those daydreams a reality. Let's explore the strategies that turn looking busy into an art form.

EIGHT

How to "Look Busy" While Procrastinating

Ah, the noble art of looking busy—a skill so subtle and yet so crucial, it deserves its own spot on your résumé. There's a certain satisfaction in mastering the illusion of productivity, a way of saying to the world, *"I'm totally working, even if I just spent ten minutes debating the ethics of pineapple on pizza."* But let's be honest: we've all had those moments when procrastination sneaks up, and you find yourself needing to look like you've got everything under control.

This chapter isn't about deception (okay, maybe a little). It's about the art of crafting a believable façade of busyness while secretly giving your brain the space it needs to recharge or daydream about winning an imaginary Nobel Prize. Whether you're dodging a meeting, avoiding an email, or buying time for your genius ideas to marinate, we'll explore foolproof ways to look like the hardest worker in the room—even if you're just mastering the perfect way to fold a napkin. Let's turn procrastination into performance art!

Lighthearted Strategies for Appearing Busy During Procrastination

Looking busy is an art form requiring practice, confidence, and just the right amount of flair. It's not about fooling people—it's about giving yourself space to procrastinate without raising eyebrows. Whether you're dodging a daunting task or buying time for inspiration to strike, these strategies will help you look like a productivity wizard, even if your main achievement is organizing your snack drawer.

Let's start with the MVP of appearing busy: keyboard clattering. Few things say, *"I'm deep in thought,"* like the rhythmic tapping of keys. It doesn't matter what you're typing—a grocery list, an apology email to your plants, or a stream-of-consciousness rant about the lack of good bagels in your area. The trick is to pause occasionally, squint at the screen as if you've cracked a major code, and sigh dramatically. Bonus points if you shake your head in frustration because nothing says *"hard at work"* like battling invisible problems.

Next, there's the legendary "strategic walk." Grab a notebook, an empty mug, or even a stapler, and stride purposefully through your workspace. Walk briskly, occasionally glancing at your watch or furrowing your brow, like you're solving a global crisis. The key is to look focused yet approachable. If someone asks what you're doing, respond with something vague but important-sounding, like *"Just following up on a few things."* No one will question it, and you'll be free to procrastinate in peace.

For the ultimate cover, there's the "fake meeting." Block off an hour on your calendar with a title like *"Team Review"* or *"Strategic Insights."* Pop in your earbuds, stare intently at your screen, and nod occasionally as though someone is dropping wisdom. You can use this sacred time to doodle, plan your imaginary vacation, or figure out what oat milk is really about. To sell it, scribble a few notes or say "good point" under your breath. You'll look so busy that no one will dare interrupt.

When procrastination strikes, physical tasks are your best friend. Tidy your desk, rearrange office supplies, or pretend to organize files. Not only does this project an aura of productivity, but it also creates a cleaner space that makes you feel like you're accomplishing something—without actually doing anything of consequence. If anyone asks, you're "streamlining your workflow," which sounds much better than *"I couldn't face my inbox."*

Speaking of which, emails are a procrastinator's playground. Reply to that message from three weeks ago asking how your weekend was, or throw a "Thanks, looks great!" into a group thread. These tiny tasks take minimal effort but make you seem engaged. Just be careful not to trigger a reply-all storm—it's a fine line between looking productive and causing chaos.

If you're working at a computer, spreadsheets are an absolute lifesaver. Open one up, fill it with random data, and maybe toss in a pie chart for good measure. Occasionally furrow your brow and adjust a cell while muttering, *"That's odd..."* Nobody will dare disturb your critical "analysis." Whether you're actually crunching numbers or just deciding your favorite types of pie, the effect is the same: pure genius at work.

Sometimes, the simplest tricks are the most effective. A well-timed sigh and distant gaze can suggest you're grappling with a monumental challenge. If someone approaches, just say, *"This project is more complex than I expected,"* or *"I'm trying to make sense of these numbers."* These vague statements stop most people from probing further, giving you more time to perfect your procrastination craft.

Finally, there's the "dual-screen illusion." Keep one screen open to a work-related document while the other holds your fun distractions. If you're quick on the keyboard, you can toggle between tabs faster than a kid switching from cartoons to homework when mom walks in.

These strategies are simple, effective, and, most importantly, amusing. They let you procrastinate with flair while maintaining the illusion of productivity. And once you've mastered the art of appearing busy, the next step is embracing simple tasks that feel like progress—even if they're just tiny pebbles on the mountain of your to-do list. After all, why climb the mountain when you can rearrange the rocks?

Simple Tasks That Feel Productive but Don't Require Real Work

The beauty of simple tasks lies in their ability to make you feel accomplished while barely breaking a mental sweat. They're the perfect solution when you need to procrastinate with flair—small enough to avoid overwhelming you but significant enough to appear like you're conquering your day. These tasks are the unsung heroes of productive procrastination, designed to make you look busy without actually tackling anything too taxing.

Let's start with a classic: tidying your workspace. Cleaning your desk, aligning your pens, or wiping down your keyboard with laser-focused precision can give the impression that you're getting ready to dive into something monumental. The reality? You're just avoiding that spreadsheet. For an added layer of pseudo-productivity, consider reorganizing your drawers. Suddenly, you're not just procrastinating —you're "streamlining efficiency."

Email sorting is another procrastinator's best friend. You're not necessarily responding to emails (let's not rush into things), but sorting them into folders is a genius way to appear organized. Create labels like *"Future Reference"* or *"Things I'll Pretend to Read Later,"* and bask in the satisfaction of clicking and dragging your way to an inbox that looks under control. If you're feeling extra ambitious, respond to one innocuous email from months ago with a quick *"Thanks for following up on this!"* You'll seem attentive, even if you completely forgot what the original email was about.

Updating your to-do list is a goldmine of low-pressure productivity. Write down tasks you've already completed just to cross them off. (*"Wake up: done. Drink coffee: nailed it."*) It's not about tackling real work—it's about creating a visual representation of your competence. Sprinkle in a few vague items like *"brainstorm strategy"* or *"review opportunities."* These sound impressive, but they don't actually require immediate action.

Digital decluttering is another top-tier task. Reorganize your desktop icons, rename random files, or delete screenshots of things you no longer remember saving. While this might not bring you closer to completing your big project, it creates the illusion that you're laying the groundwork for something huge. If anyone asks, tell them you're "optimizing your digital workspace for maximum efficiency." It's a statement that is so nonspecific that no one will challenge it.

Physical tasks offer another great opportunity to procrastinate with purpose. Rearrange your bookshelves, alphabetize your snack stash, or fold the pile of blankets in your office. These activities are mindless enough to be relaxing but still give off a productive vibe. If questioned, explain that you're clearing clutter to make space for "creative energy."

Socializing can also double as a productivity façade. Drop by a coworker's desk, or if you're working remotely, start a lighthearted chat. Begin with something neutral like, *"Just wanted to check in on that thing,"* and let the conversation naturally drift into safer procrastination territory. By the end, you'll have bonded over last weekend's TV shows while looking like a team player.

Coffee or water breaks are a perfect way to interrupt your day without raising eyebrows. Walk slowly to the kitchen with a thoughtful expression, pour your drink with intention, and maybe even pause to stare out the window as if contemplating life's deeper questions. Return to your desk looking refreshed and ready—whether or not you actually start working is beside the point.

For the ultimate in simple, productive-looking tasks, there's the legendary Paper Shuffle. Spread a few documents across your desk, pick one up with a serious expression, and occasionally tap the stack to align the edges. Mutter phrases like, *"This is interesting"* or *"That's worth noting"* to complete the act. To anyone watching, you're clearly deep in important work—when, in reality, you're probably debating what to order for lunch.

These small tasks aren't about fooling anyone—they're about giving yourself the mental space to avoid larger tasks without spiraling into unproductive guilt. Once you've mastered the art of low-stakes activity, the next step is embracing "almost finished" as an acceptable milestone. Let's explore how to celebrate progress without letting perfectionism slow you down.

Tips for Managing Appearances in Work Environments

Appearing productive is an art form, a delicate balance of looking engaged while occasionally thinking about what's for dinner. Whether you're in an office, working remotely, or balancing your laptop on a wobbly café table, managing appearances ensures you stay in everyone's good graces—even when your to-do list is mostly untouched. It's all about small moves, clever props, and the occasional furrowed brow to sell the illusion.

Body language is your first and most essential tool. Sit upright, but not like you're auditioning for a posture campaign. A slight lean forward with occasional nodding says, *"I'm in the zone,"* without looking overzealous. Add a furrowed brow when staring at your screen, as if you're decoding ancient scrolls, not debating between tacos or pizza for lunch. Tap the keyboard periodically, even if you're typing, *"Is this thing on?"* Your hands moving means productivity—or so they'll think.

Mastering eye contact is critical. If someone walks by, glance up briefly, give a slight nod, then snap back to your screen. It's the *"I acknowledge you, but my work is too important to stop"* move. If you're remote, this translates to occasionally looking at your webcam during video calls, paired with a thoughtful head tilt. For maximum effect, unmute yourself now and then to say, *"That's a great point,"* whether you've been paying attention or not.

In-office environments offer great opportunities to showcase your *I'm definitely working* vibe. The strategic walk is a classic: grab a clipboard, a mug, or literally anything that looks official, and walk briskly through the space. Keep your expression neutral but focused, as though you're solving a supply chain crisis. If someone stops you, just mutter, *"On my way to handle something,"* and keep moving. Remote workers can mimic this by shuffling papers audibly during calls, creating a subtle background symphony of competence.

Desk props also help maintain appearances. Keep sticky notes or a notebook nearby, and occasionally scribble something like *"Synergy"* or *"Optimize plan."* Pair this with a slow nod or a brief sigh, signaling you're deep in thought. If you're feeling bold, underline random words for no reason—it's the universal sign of strategic planning. A coffee cup or water bottle is another must-have. Regularly sipping from it while staring into the middle distance creates the illusion of deep problem-solving. Bonus points if you refill it dramatically, walking with a sense of purpose to the kitchen and back.

For those working remotely, the background matters. A bookshelf, a plant, and a neutral wall say, *"I'm a grounded professional."* No plants? No problem. Blur your background to create mystery—

people will assume you're hiding trade secrets, not piles of laundry. During calls, lean into the mute-unmute dance. Mute when you're "thinking" and unmute just in time to say, *"I'd like to add to that,"* even if you're just paraphrasing someone else.

Technology is your ultimate sidekick. Keep multiple tabs open to look swamped. If someone catches a glimpse of your screen, the sight of charts or graphs will do wonders—even if one tab is a BuzzFeed quiz titled *"Which Sandwich Are You?"* On video calls, use screen sharing to show off a spreadsheet. Nobody needs to know it's just you reorganizing your list of potential dog names.

Sound cues are underappreciated in the art of looking busy. A light *"hmm"* or an occasional sigh suggests you're grappling with weighty matters. Add a murmured, *"This is tricky..."* and people will leave you alone to "work." If you're remote, the mute button becomes your shield. Toggle it periodically, as if you're multi-tasking furiously between the call and urgent work.

Finally, the pièce de résistance: the deep thought pause. Sit back, cross your arms, and gaze into the distance like you're solving productivity's greatest riddle. If someone asks what's on your mind, reply, *"Just thinking through the project strategy."* It's vague enough to avoid follow-ups and confident enough to impress.

With these moves, you'll master the art of appearing busy in any work setting. Once you've nailed the illusion, it's time to take guilt-free breaks. Let's explore how to embrace downtime without worrying about what others think.

A Humorous Guide to Avoiding Judgment for Taking Breaks

Breaks are an essential part of any productive day, but the trick is taking them without attracting side-eye from coworkers—or worse, from your own inner critic. Whether you're recharging with a coffee, stretching your legs, or watching your 23rd dog video of the morning, the key is to make your breaks look intentional and necessary. Here's how to enjoy your downtime without the guilt.

Confidence is your greatest ally. A break only looks suspicious if you act like you're sneaking off to raid the cookie jar. Walk to the kitchen with purpose, mug in hand, as though refilling your coffee is the linchpin of your next big idea. If someone asks why you're on your third cup, just say, *"Fueling innovation!"* and smile knowingly. Bonus points if you return to your desk with an extra folder or notebook, as if you've been multitasking your way through groundbreaking discoveries.

For remote workers, the "intentional camera-off move" is a lifesaver. Say, *"Excuse me for just a moment,"* turn off your video, and disappear into the void. Use this precious time to grab a snack, hug your dog, or ponder the mysteries of disappearing socks. When you return, look refreshed, as though you've just solved a major work crisis, even if you were actually debating whether peanut butter counts as dinner.

If you prefer breaks that stay close to your workspace, try the strategic stretch. Stand up, reach for the sky, and let out a satisfied sigh. Pair this with a comment like, *"This project's really taking it out of me!"* to signal that you've been working so hard even your muscles are crying for relief. This move works in offices and at home—it's universally recognized as the stretch of someone deep in the grind.

The "deep thought break" is another classic. Grab a notebook and wander to a window or quiet corner. Stare out into the distance with a pensive look, occasionally jotting down something—anything. You could write *"ideas"* or *"unicorns."* No one will ask to see what you're writing because they'll assume you're brainstorming brilliance. Really, you're just mentally replaying last night's TV show finale.

Snack breaks can also be elevated into the realm of productive-looking activities. Carry your snack with you as you walk around or back to your desk, maybe balancing it with a notebook or your phone. If someone glances your way, nod at them and say, *"I'm just mulling over the next steps."* To them, you're someone multitasking snacks and strategy; to you, you're just making sure you don't drop the chips.

For office workers, the timeless "random walkabout" is a break in disguise. Hold something official-looking—a stack of papers, a coffee mug, or even a stapler—and walk purposefully from one end of the office to the other. Occasionally glance at your watch or phone to add a sense of urgency. It looks like you're juggling deadlines when, in reality, you're getting your steps in.

Remote workers have their version of this: the "mute-and-mime." Mute yourself during a video call and occasionally gesture at your screen like you're collaborating with someone. Meanwhile, stretch, grab some water, or check Instagram. When you unmute, toss in a casual *"I was just reviewing the document,"* and you're back in the game.

If anyone dares to question your breaks, bring out the trump card: health. *"Studies show stepping away for a moment boosts productivity!"* Mention how sitting too long is linked to back pain or other random health facts you vaguely remember. Nobody argues with wellness— it's the ultimate excuse.

Breaks aren't just about recharging; they're an art form. With confidence, a few props, and a touch of creativity, you can enjoy guilt-free pauses while keeping up appearances. Once you master the balance of downtime and productivity, it's time to dive into embracing progress by celebrating "almost finished" as a milestone worth cheering.

NINE

Embracing "Almost Finished" as Progress

There's a universal truth about overachievers: we're experts at turning simple tasks into epic quests. That five-slide presentation? Suddenly, it needs to rival the Gettysburg Address. The email to your boss? Why not treat it like a Pulitzer submission? But here's the thing: perfectionism is exhausting, and sometimes, "almost finished" is not just good enough—it's a victory worth celebrating.

This chapter is dedicated to breaking the chains of never-ending tinkering and embracing the magic of calling things *done-ish*. We'll dive into strategies for silencing that inner voice that insists you *could do more* and replacing it with a proud, *"Look at all I've accomplished!"* After all, progress beats paralysis every time. So, grab your nearly polished project, let's celebrate its imperfections, and move on with a smile—preferably before you decide to reformat it for the fifth time.

Learning to Stop Before Perfection and Appreciate "Good Enough"

Let's face it—perfectionism is a sneaky villain in the productivity story. It disguises itself as "high standards" or "giving your best effort," but in reality, it's the reason you've spent 45 minutes debating whether a slide should be navy blue or *slightly darker* navy blue. The truth is, sometimes good enough is not only okay—it's the only way to keep moving forward without losing your mind.

The first step to escaping the perfectionism trap is to recognize when it's happening. You know the signs: you've been editing the same paragraph for hours, rearranging words like you're trying to crack a secret code. Or maybe you've tweaked a spreadsheet until it's so color-coded it could double as modern art. Perfectionism loves these rabbit holes, and if you're not careful, you'll spend all your time "polishing" instead of finishing.

To combat this, try asking yourself a simple question: *"Will this really matter in six months?"* If the answer is no, stop. That email doesn't need a revolutionary opening line. The report doesn't need to be formatted like a designer's portfolio. Sometimes, the most impressive thing you can do is hit "send" and move on. Think of it as a mic drop moment—but with fewer dramatic exits and more quiet relief.

One of perfectionism's greatest tricks is convincing you that everyone else is scrutinizing your work as much as you are. Spoiler alert: they're not. Most people skim. Your audience isn't counting the number of bullet points on your slide deck or obsessing over your choice of fonts. (Unless your font is Comic Sans. Then, well, they might.) People care about the message, not whether you used an em dash or a hyphen. Save yourself the stress and let the tiny details go.

A great way to ease into the "good enough" mindset is to set a timer. Give yourself a fixed amount of time to complete a task, and when the timer dings, you're done—no exceptions. It's like a productivity game show: *You have 15 minutes to finish this email. No lifelines. No second drafts. Go!* Not only does this force you to prioritize the essentials, but it also teaches you that the world doesn't implode when you turn in work that's 90% perfect instead of 110%.

Another powerful tool is the "80/20 Rule," also known as the Pareto Principle. It states that 80% of results come from 20% of effort. That means most of your perfectionist tweaks—the rearranging, the fine-tuning, the triple-checking—add very little value. So, focus on the 20% that matters and let the rest go. Your future self will thank you, especially when you realize how much time you saved not arguing with yourself about semicolons.

Of course, letting go of perfectionism doesn't mean settling for sloppy. It's about finding the sweet spot between effort and efficiency. Instead of aiming for flawless, aim for "functional." For instance, if you're preparing a presentation, make sure it's clear and gets the job done—but resist the urge to spend an hour making animations smoother. It's a slide deck, not *Cirque du Soleil.*

Celebrate the victories in "almost finished." Wrap up a task, give yourself a pat on the back, and resist the urge to revisit it. If it's helpful, remind yourself that even some of history's greatest achievements weren't perfect. The Leaning Tower of Pisa? Still leaning. Mona Lisa? No eyebrows. Yet somehow, they've done just fine.

Finally, don't underestimate the power of delegating. If perfectionism has you stuck, hand off the final touches to someone else. Not only does this free up your time, but it also ensures you don't spend another hour debating font sizes. Collaboration can be a lifesaver—and sometimes, other people's "good enough" is more than enough.

In the end, progress beats perfection every time. By learning to let go, you free yourself to tackle new challenges without getting bogged down in endless revisions. And once you've embraced "good enough," it's time to face another perfectionism foe: the sneaky self-doubt that creeps in when goals start feeling unattainable. Let's dive into managing those doubts and keeping momentum alive.

Tips for Managing Self-Doubt and Releasing Unattainable Goals

Self-doubt is like an annoying backseat driver—it's loud, unhelpful, and never fails to pipe up at the worst times. *"Are you sure you're qualified for this?"* it asks as you confidently type an email. *"What if everyone hates this idea?"* it wonders while you're halfway through a presentation. The truth is, self-doubt doesn't care about your progress—it just wants to keep you second-guessing forever. But here's the good news: you don't have to let it take the wheel.

The first step in managing self-doubt is calling it out. When that inner critic shows up with its greatest hits playlist of insecurity— *"You're not ready!" "This could be better!" "What if it's terrible?"*— take a moment to recognize what's happening. Self-doubt is like a karaoke singer who's overstayed their welcome. Sure, it had its moment, but it's time to cut the mic and move on.

One trick is to reframe those doubts as harmless overreactions. For example, when your brain says, *"This isn't good enough!"* respond with, *"Oh, calm down, it's an email, not a Nobel Prize submission."* Humor disarms self-doubt faster than you'd think. By treating it as a dramatic but ultimately silly voice, you can strip it of its power and get back to work.

Another strategy is to remind yourself of your past wins. Self-doubt has a bad habit of making you forget everything you've already achieved. Keep a "brag file" with kind feedback, completed projects, or even that one time someone said, *"Great job!"* Revisit it when doubt creeps in. Think of it as your personal highlight reel, designed to drown out the inner critic with a round of applause.

Let's talk about the art of releasing unattainable goals. This is where self-doubt often thrives, whispering things like, *"You haven't finished that huge, overcomplicated project yet. What's wrong with you?"* The solution? Cut the cord. If a goal has morphed into an unmanageable monster, it's okay to let it go—or at least scale it down. Not every idea is meant to be a masterpiece. Sometimes, it's enough to say, *"This doesn't fit right now, and that's okay."*

A helpful tool here is the "priority audit." Take a hard look at your goals and ask, *"Do I still care about this, or am I holding on because it feels wrong to quit?"* If the answer is the latter, consider letting it go. It's not failure; it's making room for goals that actually excite you. Marie Kondo your ambitions: if it doesn't spark joy (or serve a purpose), thank it and move on.

When self-doubt insists you'll regret letting something go, remind yourself of all the things you've already released without disaster striking. You stopped caring about memorizing state capitals, learning the recorder, or mastering cursive. Look at you now—thriving without *"My Heart Will Go On"* on a plastic flute. Life goes on.

Another sneaky way to quiet self-doubt is to imagine the worst-case scenario. What if your project isn't perfect? What if someone critiques your work? Spoiler alert: you'll survive. Rarely does a typo or a less-than-perfect outcome result in the world ending. Most people won't even notice, let alone judge. And those who do? They're probably too busy doubting their own work to dwell on yours.

Surrounding yourself with supportive people also helps. Share your doubts with someone you trust—they'll often point out how ridiculous they sound. *"Wait, you think you're not good at this? You literally ran the whole project last quarter!"* Sometimes, hearing someone else dismiss your doubts is the fastest way to do it yourself.

Finally, embrace the mantra: *Done is better than perfect.* Self-doubt loves to stall you with perfectionist fantasies, but finishing something, even imperfectly, is always better than never starting—or worse, starting and endlessly tweaking until your sanity gives out. Celebrate your progress, no matter how small, and remind yourself that every step forward silences doubt a little more.

Once you've learned to manage self-doubt and let go of unattainable goals, it's time to focus on celebrating what you've already accomplished. Let's dive into the art of recognizing progress—even when it feels like you're moving at a snail's pace.

Celebrating Progress Rather Than Obsessing Over Completion

Celebrating progress often takes a backseat to obsessing over perfection. Instead of pausing to say, *"Wow, I've done so much!"* we zoom in on the tiniest details, wondering if the bullet points on slide three should be indented more. Here's the truth: perfection is overrated. Progress is what keeps the world spinning—and it's high time you gave yourself some credit.

Start by remembering that most people won't notice the details you're agonizing over. You're the only one keeping track of whether that paragraph is 98% perfect or 100% flawless. Your audience? They're just happy they didn't have to write it. If the report makes sense, the slides are legible, and the big picture shines through, congratulations—you've nailed it. Stop acting like the fate of humanity depends on whether your pie chart has exactly three shades of blue.

Shifting your focus to milestones instead of the finish line can be a game-changer. Milestones are like pit stops—they let you refuel and celebrate without needing to collapse at the end. Did you finish a rough draft? High-five yourself. Wrote half an email? Reward yourself with a quick coffee break. Progress isn't about doing it all at once—it's about moving forward one step at a time, and those steps deserve to be celebrated.

If you're struggling to see your progress, try asking yourself, *"Would Past Me be impressed?"* Look back to when you started the task, staring blankly at a blank screen, wondering how to begin. Now, you've got a draft, a few solid ideas, or at least an outline. Past You would be over the moon. Give yourself credit for how far you've come—it's a lot further than you think.

A visual reminder of your progress can also work wonders. Make a checklist or chart where you can track what you've accomplished. Every ticked box or crossed-off item is proof that you're getting there. Whether it's a list on your desk or a digital tracker on your phone, seeing progress laid out in front of you can boost your motivation. Even if the first item is *"Start something,"* checking it off feels amazing.

Perfectionists, this one's for you: aiming for "done" instead of "perfect" is not settling—it's smart. Spending hours fine-tuning every little detail won't always add value; it just drains your energy. Most tasks don't need to be flawless—they just need to be functional. Your slide deck doesn't have to belong in a design competition. Your email doesn't need to win a Pulitzer. It just needs to get the job done.

Don't underestimate the power of celebrating small wins. Did you write one sentence? Fantastic—it's one more sentence than you had before. Did you brainstorm for 10 minutes before getting distracted by your phone? That's 10 solid minutes of effort. Treat every tiny step as a reason to celebrate, even if it's just a fist pump and a muttered, *"Go me!"*

Avoid falling into the comparison trap. Sure, someone else might have finished their project faster or made their work shinier, but that doesn't mean your progress is less valuable. For all you know, they stayed up all night fueled by energy drinks and existential dread. Everyone works at their own pace. Celebrate your progress on your terms.

Finally, learn to recognize when something is "done enough." If your project meets the requirements, checks the main boxes, and doesn't have glaring errors, let it go. Use the time you'd spend obsessing over tweaks to reward yourself with something fun—watch a show, take a walk, or nap like a champion. Progress deserves celebration, not endless second-guessing.

By focusing on progress rather than perfection, you'll not only save yourself time but also keep your momentum strong. Once you've embraced this mindset, you'll be ready to tackle deadlines with ease —turning them from stress-filled enemies into gentle guides for productivity. Let's explore how deadlines can work for you instead of against you.

Humor About the Never-Ending Pursuit of "Perfect"

Perfection is the ultimate moving target. Just when you think you've nailed it, you spot one more tweak, one more adjustment, one more *tiny improvement* that absolutely must be made before you can call it done. And that's how you end up spending 45 minutes deciding whether your font should be Arial or Calibri as if the fate of the universe hangs in the balance. Spoiler: it doesn't.

The pursuit of perfection is a bit like chasing a hamster on a wheel— you're expending a lot of energy but not really getting anywhere. Sure, it feels productive to reformat your slides for the fourth time or change "happy" to "delighted" in your email, but deep down, you know it's not moving the needle. That's perfectionism's dirty little secret: it tricks you into thinking that endless tinkering is progress when it's really procrastination in a fancy outfit.

One of perfectionism's favorite tricks is convincing you that the tiniest detail matters to everyone. *"What if they hate the alignment on this chart? What if they judge me for this comma placement?"* Here's the truth: nobody is paying that much attention. Your audience is probably skimming, half-distracted by their own to-do lists or wondering what's for lunch. That slide deck you spent hours perfecting? They're more likely to comment on the *content* than on whether you used Pantone 294 or Pantone 295 for the title bar.

A great way to keep perfectionism in check is to play the "Will Anyone Die?" game. If your project isn't perfect, will anyone die? No? Great, move on. If you're still stuck, consider the "Three Ps Rule": Is it professional? Is it presentable? Is it passable? If the answer to all three is yes, hit *send,* walk away, and bask in the glow of knowing you've outsmarted perfectionism yet again.

Another sneaky thing perfectionism does is inflate the stakes. Suddenly, finishing that email draft feels as daunting as writing a novel. When you catch yourself spiraling, take a step back and ask, *"What's the actual goal here?"* If the goal is to communicate clearly, then guess what? Your email doesn't need to be a masterpiece. It just needs to get the point across. Save your literary genius for your side hustle.

A fun strategy for combating perfectionism is to give yourself a time limit. Set a timer, and when it goes off, you're done—no more tweaking. Think of it like a productivity reality show: *"You have 30 minutes to finish this report! Go!"* By treating your task as a game, you'll stay focused on the essentials and leave the unnecessary fluff behind. Plus, when the timer dings, you'll experience the joy of being free to move on.

Here's another radical idea: *embrace imperfection.* Some of history's greatest works aren't perfect. The Leaning Tower of Pisa? Famous for being a little lopsided. Van Gogh's brushstrokes? Wildly imprecise, yet iconic. Your work doesn't have to be perfect to make an impact. Often, it's the imperfections that make things memorable—and human. So, the next time you're stressing over a minor detail, ask yourself, *"What would Van Gogh do?"* (Hopefully not cut off your ear, but you get the point.)

And don't forget to laugh at yourself. Humor is the kryptonite to perfectionism. When you catch yourself rewriting the same sentence for the fifth time, step back and say, *"Wow, look at me, acting like this email is going into the Smithsonian."* By acknowledging the absurdity of perfectionism, you take away its power.

Finally, remind yourself that perfection is overrated. Done is better than perfect, and progress is better than paralysis. Celebrate what you've accomplished, imperfections and all, and give yourself permission to move on. There's freedom in letting go—and, as you'll soon discover, deadlines are one of the best tools for keeping perfectionism in check.

Speaking of deadlines, it's time to explore how to transform them from panic-inducing monsters into helpful guides that keep you moving forward without losing your cool. Let's dive in!

TEN

Using Deadlines as Gentle Motivation

Deadlines are the sworn enemy of procrastinators everywhere, sneaking up on us like a stealthy ninja with a clipboard. They start as far-off whispers—*"You've got plenty of time!"*—and before you know it, they're screaming, *"THIS IS DUE IN TWO HOURS!"* But what if deadlines didn't have to feel like impending doom? What if they could be more like a friendly nudge from a well-meaning friend rather than a slap from reality?

In this chapter, we're going to reframe deadlines. Instead of seeing them as ticking time bombs, we'll treat them as helpful guideposts— a tool to focus your mind, manage your time, and trick yourself into action. After all, deadlines don't have to be scary. They can be the productivity fairy godmother you didn't know you needed—minus the wand and sparkles (unless you're into that). So, let's learn how to make deadlines work for you, not against you!

How to View Deadlines as Guideposts Rather Than Stress Points

Deadlines have an undeserved reputation for being terrifying. They loom ominously on calendars, taunting you like a pop quiz you forgot to study for. But the truth is, deadlines aren't out to ruin your life—they're just trying to help you get things done without binge-watching your 37th episode of "The Great British Bake Off." If you treat them right, deadlines can become helpful guideposts rather than panic-inducing monsters.

The first step to reframing deadlines is to stop thinking of them as doomsday clocks. They're not ticking toward your productivity judgment day; they're simply reminders that it's time to wrap things up. Deadlines are more like helpful road signs. If you treat them as directional markers instead of screaming alarms, you'll feel more in control—and less like you're in an action movie where the bomb timer is counting down.

One way to make deadlines friendlier is to rename them. Instead of calling them "deadlines," which sounds like something you'd see in a horror movie, call them "goal lines" or "finish lines." Finish lines are exciting. They're celebratory. People cheer at finish lines. Add a reward at the end—like a treat or an hour of guilt-free procrastination—and suddenly, deadlines feel more like a victory lap than a punishment.

Breaking down a big deadline into smaller ones is another lifesaver. If your final project is due on Friday, aim to finish one part by Wednesday, another by Thursday, and so on. This approach turns an overwhelming mountain into manageable molehills. Think of it as eating a giant cake—you don't stuff the whole thing in your mouth at once (unless it's been a rough week). You savor it one slice at a time.

If you thrive under pressure but still want to avoid last-minute chaos, set a fake deadline for yourself. Pretend the project is due a day or two before the real one. It's like tricking your inner procrastinator into thinking time is running out—without the actual panic attack. Bonus: if you meet your fake deadline, you have extra time to relax, proofread, or debate whether that last bullet point needs an asterisk.

Humor also works wonders for easing deadline stress. Rename your deadlines with ridiculous titles like *"Operation Sparkly Unicorn"* or *"Mission: Not a Dumpster Fire."* Seeing these on your calendar is guaranteed to make you laugh—and remind you that it's just work, not life or death. After all, who can stress out about something called *"Banana Pancake Tuesday"*?

Gamifying deadlines can make them less daunting, too. Set small challenges like, *"Can I finish this email draft before my tea gets cold?"* or *"Let's knock out these bullet points before the next Spotify ad plays."* Turning work into a game tricks your brain into having fun. And let's be honest, your brain loves being tricked.

When deadlines feel overwhelming, don't be afraid to ask for help. Whether it's a coworker, a friend, or the random barista who's been fueling your caffeine habit, talking things through can make deadlines less intimidating. Even if the person can't directly help, sharing the load lightens the stress. At the very least, your plant will listen attentively— and maybe even offer moral support with its unwavering green presence.

Finally, celebrate progress along the way. Finished a section early? Dance break. Hit a mini-deadline? Reward yourself with a donut— or, let's be real, two donuts. Even if you're still working toward the big deadline, those small wins deserve recognition. They remind you that you're making strides, not just spinning in circles.

Deadlines aren't out to get you—they're just nudging you toward finishing what you started. By treating them as friendly finish lines rather than looming threats, you can make progress without the pressure. And speaking of progress, let's talk about creating mini-deadlines to keep that momentum going strong, one manageable step at a time.

Creating Mini-Deadlines for Smaller Accomplishments

Mini-deadlines are like deadlines' cooler, more approachable cousins. They don't barge into your calendar shouting, *"Finish everything now!"* Instead, they gently whisper, *"How about just this one little thing?"* By breaking big tasks into smaller chunks, mini-deadlines help you stay on track without the overwhelming pressure of tackling everything at once. They're the snack-sized candy bars of productivity—delightfully manageable and just as satisfying.

The beauty of mini-deadlines lies in their simplicity. Instead of staring at a massive project due in two weeks, break it into smaller tasks with their own "due dates." For example, if you're writing a report, set a mini-deadline for finishing the introduction by Monday, the body by Wednesday, and the conclusion by Friday. Suddenly, it's not one giant project—it's a series of bite-sized wins. And let's be honest, who doesn't love a win, no matter how small?

To make mini-deadlines work, start with realistic goals. Don't promise yourself you'll write ten pages in an hour unless you have supernatural typing skills or a time machine. Aim for something achievable, like drafting one section or even outlining your ideas. The smaller the goal, the more likely you are to accomplish it—and the less likely you are to spend the next hour Googling whether sloths ever sneeze (they do).

Using timers can also turn mini-deadlines into a fun, low-stress game. Set a timer for 25 minutes (hello, Pomodoro technique) and challenge yourself to finish a specific task before it dings. There's something oddly motivating about racing against the clock, especially if you pretend you're in a high-stakes action movie where completing your email draft somehow saves the day. Bonus points if you hum a dramatic soundtrack while you work.

Another trick is to tie your mini-deadlines to natural breaks in your day. For instance, tell yourself you'll finish editing a section before lunch or draft an outline before your next coffee refill. These time anchors create a sense of urgency without feeling oppressive. Plus, they give you built-in rewards—because nothing makes a sandwich taste better than knowing you've earned it by slaying your morning to-do list.

Accountability partners can also boost the power of mini-deadlines. Share your small goals with a friend, coworker, or unsuspecting pet. Saying, *"I'll finish this by 3 p.m."* out loud makes it harder to let the task slide. If your accountability buddy is a person, ask them to check in on your progress. If it's a pet, well, they'll just stare at you judgmentally—but that's surprisingly effective motivation, too.

One of the best things about mini-deadlines is how flexible they are. Miss one? No big deal—adjust and move on. Unlike big deadlines, which tend to cause full-blown panic if you fall behind, mini-deadlines are forgiving. They're like the chill friend who doesn't mind rescheduling brunch when life gets in the way. Just make sure you're not using their flexibility as an excuse to push everything to "later." Mini-deadlines should keep you moving forward, not perpetually kicking the can down the road.

Celebrate every time you hit a mini-deadline. Whether it's a quick high-five with yourself or a victory lap around the office (or your living room), acknowledging these small wins keeps you motivated. Treat yourself to a coffee, a cookie, or even five glorious minutes of scrolling through memes guilt-free. These little celebrations reinforce the idea that progress is worth cheering for, even when the final deadline is still on the horizon.

Mini-deadlines aren't just about productivity—they're about preserving your sanity. They take the weight of a massive task off your shoulders and replace it with manageable pieces that actually feel doable. By focusing on one step at a time, you'll not only reduce your stress but also build momentum toward that big finish.

Once you've mastered the art of mini-deadlines, it's time to shift gears and explore the relationship between urgency and panic. Let's talk about how to manage those last-minute rushes without losing your cool—or your sense of humor.

Humor About Procrastinator-Friendly Deadline Adjustments

Deadlines are supposed to be fixed points in time, but if you're a seasoned procrastinator, you know they're more like polite suggestions. *"The 15th?"* you ask yourself. *"Why not the 18th? What's a few days between friends?"* Adjusting deadlines is practically a sport for procrastinators—a delicate dance of negotiation, creativity, and sheer optimism that time will somehow bend to your will.

One of the classic procrastinator moves is the *self-imposed deadline adjustment.* This happens when you think, *"I'll start two weeks early, so I have plenty of time!"* Then, one week in, you realize the only thing you've started is a deep dive into ranking the best donuts of all time (Boston Cream, obviously). At this point, your brain kicks in with its trademark flexibility: *"I didn't mean two weeks early. I meant two days early!"* And just like that, your timeline shifts with zero guilt. Genius.

Another hallmark of deadline adjustment is the *unexpected life crisis.* This is when you suddenly discover you absolutely cannot finish your task because something "urgent" has come up. Maybe it's a "family emergency," like teaching your grandma to use Instagram filters. Or perhaps your dog has suddenly decided today is the day to bark at every leaf in the yard, and you're now stuck in canine mediation. Whatever the excuse, you convince yourself the delay is entirely justified—and hey, deadlines are flexible, right?

For professionals, the *"collaborative extension"* is a classic. It's when you casually bring up the idea of a later deadline during a meeting: *"Wouldn't it be better for everyone if we had a few more days to make this really shine?"* Bonus points if you frame it as being considerate to the team, as though the extra time is a selfless act of generosity. Your coworkers will appreciate it—or at least pretend to—while you quietly revel in your newfound breathing room.

Procrastinators also excel at *creative prioritization,* a fancy way of saying, *"I'll do literally anything else before this."* Faced with a looming deadline, you suddenly remember that you haven't reorganized your sock drawer since 2017. Clearly, the task can't wait another minute. But don't worry—you justify it by convincing yourself that a well-organized sock drawer will lead to unparalleled focus, making the actual deadline a breeze.

There's also the *overestimated efficiency adjustment.* This is when you tell yourself, *"I work best under pressure!"* and decide to start the night before. You imagine yourself in a montage of peak productivity —typing furiously, coffee steaming, inspirational music swelling in the background. Reality? You're staring at a blank screen at midnight, Googling *"how to write fast"* while debating if it's too late to switch careers entirely.

Humor aside, the trick to deadline adjustments is knowing your limits. While it's fun to push the boundaries of "on time," there's a fine line between buying yourself extra breathing room and spiraling into chaos. If you're going to shift a deadline, make it intentional—decide how much time you need and stick to it. Procrastinators thrive on last-minute magic, but even magic needs a plan.

Here's a hot tip: use the *"fake deadline"* approach to outsmart yourself. Tell your brain the task is due a day or two earlier than it actually is. Your inner procrastinator will believe it, and when the real deadline arrives, you'll already be done—or at least close enough to avoid panic mode. It's like a Jedi mind trick for time management.

Finally, remember to laugh at the absurdity of it all. Procrastinator-friendly deadline adjustments may not always be efficient, but they're nothing if not creative. The important thing is to keep moving forward, even if you're sidestepping along the way. And when that deadline finally hits, you'll find a way to make it happen—because procrastinators, for all their delays, are masters of the last-minute save.

Now that you've mastered the art of deadline adjustments let's talk about managing urgency itself. We'll explore how to tackle pressing tasks without losing your cool—or your procrastination flair.

Tips for Managing Urgency Without Panic

Urgency has a way of turning even the calmest person into a deer in headlights. One minute, you're leisurely scrolling through cat memes, and the next, you're realizing that report is due in three hours, and you've written exactly zero words. The key to surviving these moments isn't superhuman productivity—it's learning how to stay cool under pressure while pretending you totally had this planned all along.

Step one: breathe. Seriously. When urgency hits, your first instinct might be to flail wildly, throw papers in the air, and declare yourself a lost cause. Instead, take a moment to inhale deeply and convince yourself that this isn't a disaster—it's a challenge. Channel your inner action hero. You're not panicking; you're just moving into "high-stakes efficiency mode." Bonus points if you hum a dramatic soundtrack while you work.

Once you've collected yourself, break the task down into bite-sized pieces. It's tempting to look at the whole looming project and think,

"There's no way I can do all this in time!" But by focusing on one small task at a time—write an outline, draft the intro, pretend you know what you're doing—you can chip away at the urgency without feeling completely overwhelmed. It's like eating an elephant one bite at a time, except way less gross.

Prioritize ruthlessly. When time is running out, not everything can get done, and that's okay. Identify the most important parts of the task—the pieces that will have the biggest impact or are absolutely non-negotiable—and focus on those. The less critical stuff? It can wait or disappear entirely. It's triage for your to-do list, and you're the calm doctor making the tough calls.

If you're really pressed for time, embrace the art of the *"quick and dirty"* solution. This isn't the moment for perfectionism or overthinking. Write that email, create that slide, or answer that question with just enough effort to get it done. Remember, sometimes *done* is better than *perfect.* Nobody is handing out medals for the best-designed spreadsheet at 11:59 p.m.

Use timers to stay focused. Set a short countdown—15 or 20 minutes—and challenge yourself to work on just one part of the task. This "sprint" approach keeps your brain from wandering into *"what if I Googled penguins for five minutes?"* territory. When the timer goes off, give yourself a quick break (yes, Googling penguins is fine here) before diving into the next chunk of work. Urgency thrives on momentum, and these mini-deadlines keep you moving forward.

Don't be afraid to ask for help if you need it. Urgent situations can sometimes make you feel like a lone warrior battling a horde of angry deadlines, but there's no shame in calling for backup. A coworker, a friend, or even that one super-organized person in your office who alphabetizes their sticky notes might have ideas, insights, or support to make your task easier. Collaboration is not a sign of weakness; it's a productivity hack.

Finally, keep a sense of humor about the whole situation. Urgency is temporary, and when it's all over, you'll have a great story about the time you threw together a last-minute presentation that didn't just meet expectations—it crushed them. Laughing at the absurdity of it all helps you stay grounded, and it's a reminder that even under pressure, you're capable of pulling off amazing things.

Once the dust settles and the urgent task is behind you, it's time to take a step back, reflect, and plan your next move. And sometimes, that next move involves pausing to recharge. In the next chapter, we'll explore how to pause productively—because even the busiest procrastinator needs a well-earned break.

ELEVEN

Learning to "Pause" Productively

Pausing productively might sound like an oxymoron, but hear me out. You know those moments when you tell yourself, *"I'll just take a quick break,"* and suddenly it's two hours later and you've somehow become an expert on how otters hold hands while they sleep? Yeah, those pauses aren't exactly productive. But what if you could pause intentionally, recharge your brain, and come back stronger than ever—without disappearing into the abyss of random internet facts?

This chapter is all about redefining the break. We're not here to shame your snack breaks or your 87th coffee run of the day (we love snacks, too) but rather to help you turn those pauses into power moves. From creative resets to sneaky ways of making downtime feel like progress, we'll explore how to embrace the art of intentional procrastination. Because sometimes, stepping away from your work is exactly what you need to step up your game.

Building Breaks into Tasks for Perspective and Energy

Let's face it: powering through tasks without breaks is like trying to run a marathon on a steady diet of energy drinks and stubbornness. Sure, you might get far for a while, but eventually, you'll crash, burn, and wonder why you thought this was a good idea. Breaks, when done right, are the secret weapon of productivity—they keep your brain sharp, your creativity flowing, and your sanity intact. Plus, they give you a guilt-free excuse to step away from your work for a bit.

The trick to productive breaks is to build them into your tasks instead of waiting until you're on the verge of collapse. Think of breaks as little brain snacks, keeping your mental energy fueled throughout the day. If you're working on a big project, divide it into chunks, and take a quick break after each one. Write a paragraph, take a breather. Finish a slide, grab a coffee. Draft a brilliant email, reward yourself with a YouTube video of baby pandas falling over. Your brain will thank you.

Timers are your best friend when it comes to structured breaks. Set a timer for 25 minutes, work like a focused genius during that time, and then reward yourself with a five-minute break. (Yes, this is the Pomodoro Technique. No, it doesn't involve tomatoes, but feel free to eat one if it helps.) Those short bursts of work and rest keep you in the zone without frying your circuits.

If you're someone who feels guilty about taking breaks, reframe them as "strategic resets." That sounds fancy and responsible—like something you'd hear at a TED Talk. When you pause to stretch, sip tea, or even stare out the window like a moody poet, you're not wasting time. You're giving your brain the space it needs to process ideas, solve problems, and recharge for the next round.

And let's not forget about the *power walk*. Taking a stroll, even if it's just a lap around your office or living room, is a perfect way to break up tasks. Walking boosts creativity, helps you think through problems, and lets you pretend you're in a montage from an inspirational movie. For added effect, hum a motivational tune while pacing. Congratulations—you're the star of *Procrastinator's Redemption.*

If you're at a desk all day, physical movement is your break-time MVP. Stretch your arms, do a few squats, or shake out your legs like you're preparing for the 100-meter dash (even if the only thing you're sprinting to is the kitchen for snacks). Movement wakes up your body and clears your mind. Bonus: it gives you an excuse to show off your "athletic" side without having to commit to an actual workout.

Breaks can also be an opportunity to reset your workspace. Use a short pause to tidy up your desk, clear out your email clutter, or finally deal with that teetering pile of sticky notes that looks like a Leaning Tower of Chaos. A clean, organized space can feel like a fresh start—and it makes you look like you've got your life together, even if your break activity was actually just hiding the mess in a drawer.

For the ultimate in productive pausing, try a "mini-meditation." Before you roll your eyes, hear me out. This doesn't mean sitting cross-legged and chanting "om" for hours. Just close your eyes for a minute, focus on your breathing, and let your brain take a mini-vacation. Think of it as a reboot for your mental hard drive. When you come back, you'll feel sharper, calmer, and less likely to curse at your next email.

The beauty of breaks is that they don't just recharge your energy—they give you perspective. Stepping away from a task lets you return with fresh eyes and better ideas. So the next time you're tempted to skip a break and push through, remember even your computer needs to restart occasionally.

Once you've mastered the art of pausing, it's time to explore how to reset your focus mid-project. Because sometimes, the only thing standing between you and productivity is a well-timed mental reset. Let's dive into how to make it happen.

Reframing Pauses as Essential to Productive Procrastination

Pauses get a bad rap. They're often seen as lazy or unmotivated moments, but in reality, they're the secret sauce to keeping your productivity fresh and your brain happy. Think of pauses as the commercial breaks during your favorite TV show: sure, you could skip them, but then when would you get up, grab snacks, and ponder life's mysteries? Just like those breaks are critical to enjoying your binge-watching session, strategic pauses are essential to surviving—and thriving—in your workday.

Let's start by calling pauses what they really are: investments. When you pause, you're not "wasting time." You're refueling your brain's creative engine so it can keep running without overheating and demanding a day-long nap. Pausing isn't about slacking off; it's about showing your brain a little TLC so it doesn't retaliate by turning your next project into a scatterbrained mess of typos and bad ideas.

The key to reframing pauses is to make them intentional. Instead of letting a pause turn into *"accidentally scrolled TikTok for 45 minutes,"* treat your break like a mini ritual. Maybe it's stepping away to make a cup of tea, standing at your window to observe the squirrels living their best lives, or taking a luxurious stretch that makes you feel like a yoga master—even if your actual flexibility is more pretzel than swan.

Pauses also work wonders for creativity. Ever notice how your best ideas pop up when you're doing something unrelated, like washing dishes or pretending to listen during a meeting? That's the magic of letting your brain wander. When you step away from a task, your subconscious takes over, connecting ideas in ways your conscious mind never could. Suddenly, that impossible project feels doable—or at least less terrifying.

If you need a productivity excuse to pause, here's a good one: pauses actually make you faster in the long run. Pushing through without stopping is like trying to drive on an empty tank. Sure, you'll keep going for a bit, but eventually, you'll sputter out and end up stranded on the side of the mental highway. A short, purposeful pause gives you the fuel you need to finish strong—and with fewer "Why did I write this sentence twice?" moments.

For the skeptics who think, *"But I don't have time to pause!"*—you're exactly the person who needs them. Pauses don't have to be elaborate. A two-minute reset can do wonders. Close your eyes, take a deep breath, and imagine your happy place. (If your happy place is a tropical beach where nobody uses "Reply All," you're not alone.) Those couple of minutes can save you from spending 20 minutes staring blankly at your screen.

Another way to make pauses feel purposeful is to combine them with light movement. Take a short walk, do some light stretches, or perform an exaggerated yawn like you're auditioning for a sitcom about overtired office workers. Moving your body while taking a mental break helps shake off the cobwebs and resets your focus. Plus, it gives you a chance to pretend you're an active, well-rounded human—even if you spend the rest of the day glued to your chair.

If you're still feeling guilty about pausing, reframe it as a "progress assessment." Use your break to reflect on what you've accomplished so far. Even if all you've done is open your email and delete three spam messages, it's progress. Give yourself a pat on the back, then use the pause to plan your next step. It's the perfect blend of rest and productivity, like the multitasking champion you are.

Finally, treat pauses as moments to savor. Instead of rushing through them or feeling bad about them, embrace the joy of not working for a few minutes. Whether it's sipping your coffee slowly, laughing at a funny meme, or zoning out to the sound of rain, let yourself enjoy the pause guilt-free. After all, pauses aren't just breaks from work—they're reminders that you're human, not a productivity robot.

Once you've mastered the art of reframing pauses, the next step is learning how to reset your focus mid-project without losing momentum. Let's explore how to hit the mental refresh button when you need it most.

How to "Reset" Mid-Project Without Losing Focus

Resetting mid-project is an underrated skill, mostly because it feels counterproductive at first. *"Reset? But I'm already behind! If I stop now, I'll never finish!"* Sound familiar? In reality, pushing through a mental fog is like trying to drive a car with a dirty windshield—you might still get there, but not without veering dangerously close to disaster. A mid-project reset isn't a setback; it's a recalibration to make sure you're heading in the right direction without crashing into procrastination potholes.

The first step to a productive reset is admitting you need one. If your brain feels like it's stuffed with cotton candy, you've reread the same sentence ten times, or you're seriously considering whether you could get away with using Comic Sans in a presentation, it's time to pause and refresh. Step away from the task and give your brain a much-needed breather—it's not quitting, it's regrouping.

One of the best ways to reset is the classic *"change your scenery"* trick. If you've been chained to your desk for hours, move to a different spot. Work from the couch, the kitchen table, or even that weird chair nobody likes. If you're at the office, relocate to the break room, a conference room, or the mythical "quiet corner." A new view can trick your brain into thinking it's starting fresh, even if all you're doing is staring at a slightly different wall.

Another effective reset technique is the *"micro-reward system."* Tell yourself, *"If I work for another 20 minutes, I can have a cookie,"* or *"Finish this section, and I get five minutes to look at pictures of baby otters."* Pairing work with small rewards turns the reset into a game. And let's be honest—everything is better with cookies and otters.

Movement is another great reset button. Stand up, stretch like you're auditioning for a yoga video, or take a quick walk. If you're feeling adventurous, do a little dance break. Nothing says *"I've got this,"* like flailing your arms to an upbeat song, even if your moves scream *"baby giraffe learning to walk."* Not only will this clear your head, but it might also make you laugh—and laughter is one of the best focus tools out there.

If your mental clutter is the problem, try a "brain dump." Grab a piece of paper or open a blank document and write down every thought swirling in your head. It doesn't matter if it's relevant to your project or just a random grocery list—getting it out of your brain clears space for the task at hand. Once it's all on paper, you'll feel like a zen master, ready to tackle that spreadsheet without wondering if you're out of oat milk.

Resetting can also mean breaking down your project into even smaller chunks. If the idea of finishing feels overwhelming, focus on a single, tiny goal. Instead of saying, *"I need to complete this report,"* tell yourself, *"Let's just outline the first section."* Smaller goals are less intimidating, and crossing them off feels just as satisfying as completing the whole thing. It's like leveling up in a video game—small victories lead to big wins.

Sometimes, a quick reset involves shifting gears entirely. Work on something else for a few minutes to give your brain a break from the task that's stumping you. Reply to a low-stakes email, organize your desk, or even Google how long turtles can hold their breath. (Spoiler: it's surprisingly long.) The key is to step back just enough to return with fresh eyes and renewed energy.

Finally, give yourself permission to restart without guilt. Resetting doesn't mean you're failing; it means you're smart enough to recognize when you're stuck. Treat it as an essential part of the process, like sharpening a pencil before writing or brewing coffee before a long day. When you reset effectively, you'll work faster, better, and with way fewer instances of yelling, *"Why is this so hard?!"*

Once you've learned to reset mid-project, the next step is discovering intentional procrastination activities that re-energize your creativity while keeping productivity in sight. Let's explore how to make those moments count.

Fun Ideas for "Intentional" Procrastination Activities

Let's be honest: not all procrastination is created equal. There's the kind where you spiral into a TikTok black hole, emerging two hours later with no idea what year it is. And then there's *intentional* procrastination—the kind that recharges your brain, sparks creativity, and somehow makes you feel like you're still sort of working. This isn't about wasting time; it's about wasting time *strategically.* Here are some fun, guilt-free ways to procrastinate with purpose.

First up: the **Desk Olympics.** Organizing your desk isn't just tidying —it's a low-key competitive event against yourself. Can you stack those sticky notes faster than last time? How many pens can you test before realizing half of them don't even work? Bonus points if you find that one ancient receipt from a coffee shop and convince yourself it's a historical artifact.

If organizing your workspace isn't your thing, there's always the **Google Quest.** Pick something tangentially related to your task and dive deep into its trivia. Writing a marketing plan? Look up the weirdest ad campaigns in history. Working on a spreadsheet? Learn about the invention of Excel (spoiler: it's probably less exciting than you think, but still). You'll feel like a detective on the trail of obscure knowledge, and you might even find a nugget of inspiration—or at least a great anecdote for the next time someone asks, *"So, what did you do today?"*

Another favorite is the **Office Safari,** where you take a stroll around your workspace (or house) to "recharge your creativity." This is your chance to inspect every plant, observe your coworkers' (or roommates') mysterious lunch choices, and maybe even discover that the office coffee machine has settings you've never dared to try. If you work from home, this might just mean wandering the kitchen, opening the fridge six times, and ultimately settling for cereal. Still counts as a safari.

For those feeling more tactile, **Creative Doodling** is the ultimate intentional procrastination activity. Grab a pen and sketch your task as if it's a comic strip or an abstract masterpiece. Are you brainstorming for a presentation? Draw it as a battle plan for world domination. Working on a budget? Sketch a pie chart that looks like an actual pie. You're still thinking about your task—just in a way that lets your brain have a little fun.

If you need to move your body, embrace the **Productivity Dance Break.** Put on your favorite playlist and dance like no one's watching. Or, if they are watching, make it a performance. It's not just procrastination; it's "boosting morale." By the time you sit back down, you'll feel re-energized and ready to tackle that next bullet point (or at least pretend to).

Another great option is the **Snack Challenge.** This isn't just eating—it's a culinary investigation. Can you make the ultimate desk snack using only what's in your kitchen or breakroom? Pair unlikely combinations, like pretzels and peanut butter or raisins and cheese. Bonus points for creating something Instagram-worthy. Just don't forget to "taste-test" as part of your research.

For the digital wanderers, there's **Email Archaeology.** Dig through your inbox and reply to those emails you swore you'd get to "later." (Remember that one from three months ago asking if you wanted to join a committee? Now's your chance to politely decline without them expecting it.) Sure, it's procrastination, but it's also clearing your digital clutter—and doesn't that feel productive?

Finally, embrace the **Productive Power Nap.** Set a timer for 15–20 minutes, close your eyes, and let your brain do some behind-the-scenes problem-solving. Napping is scientifically proven to improve focus, creativity, and your general ability to not lose it at your computer. Just make sure you don't drift into a two-hour slumber and wake up panicked about what year it is.

Intentional procrastination isn't about dodging work; it's about finding ways to recharge and refocus while keeping guilt at bay. When done right, it's less about avoidance and more about alignment—helping you come back to your task with a fresh perspective and renewed energy.

Now that you've mastered the art of purposeful pausing, let's wrap up by learning how to finish tasks without getting stuck in the endless loop of perfectionism. Because "done" really is better than "still tinkering."

TWELVE

Wrapping Up Without Getting Stuck in Perfectionism

Ah, the finish line—the glorious moment when you can finally close the laptop, check the box, or hit "send" with a triumphant flourish. Except, wait... is it really finished? Should you reread it just one more time? Maybe the conclusion could use a bit more *oomph,* and that font doesn't quite scream *"polished professional."* Before you know it, you're trapped in the endless loop of tweaking and second-guessing, like a hamster running on a wheel made entirely of self-doubt.

This chapter is all about breaking free of the "just one more edit" mindset and learning to declare a project done—without the gnawing fear that you've missed something. We'll tackle the art of letting go, celebrate the beauty of *good enough,* and, most importantly, teach you how to reward yourself for finishing (even if it's slightly imperfect). Because in the grand scheme of things, completion trumps perfection every single time.

Letting Go of the Need for Over-Editing or Endless Revisions

We've all been there: staring at a finished project, convinced it just needs *one more tweak* to make it perfect. You'll just fix that sentence, adjust the margins, and maybe spend an hour picking the perfect shade of blue for the header. Fast forward three hours, and you're knee-deep in revisions no one asked for, wondering if it's possible to over-edit yourself into oblivion. (Spoiler: it is.)

The first step to letting go of over-editing is to acknowledge the truth: nobody cares about your work as much as you do. That typo you're obsessing over? Most people won't notice it unless it's in size 72 font and blinking like a neon sign. The shade of blue you're debating? To everyone else, it's just "blue." Stop convincing yourself that your audience is a pack of eagle-eyed critics ready to pounce on every misplaced comma. Odds are, they'll skim your work and move on.

One of the sneaky ways perfectionism traps us is by whispering, *"But what if they judge you?"* Newsflash: nobody is grading your effort like a reality show judge panel. (And if they are, you're probably on the wrong show.) People value clarity and functionality far more than whether your bullet points have the exact same indentation. If your work gets the job done, you're already ahead of the game.

To escape the endless revision loop, set clear boundaries for yourself. For example: "I will review this document twice—once for content and once for typos—and then it's done." Stick to this rule like it's the last donut in the breakroom. By limiting your editing passes, you'll force yourself to focus on the big picture instead of nitpicking the details for eternity.

If you struggle to walk away from your work, try the *"Future You"* trick. Imagine Future You opening the project six months from now. Would Future You thank you for obsessively aligning every column, or would they roll their eyes and say, *"Why did Past Me waste so much time on this?"* Let Future You be your voice of reason. Spoiler: they probably don't care about the font kerning either.

Timers can also be your best friend. Set a countdown for 30 minutes and promise yourself that when it buzzes, you'll stop editing. Treat it like a competitive cooking show—when the timer hits zero, hands off! Nobody's adding more paprika to the soup, and you're not adding more words to the document. It's done whether you feel ready or not.

Another trick? Declare your project "done" to someone else. Once you've said it out loud—*"The report is finished!"*—it's harder to go back and start tinkering again. Even better, hit *send* or save before your inner perfectionist starts whispering, *"But maybe we could rewrite the conclusion..."* It's like ripping off a Band-Aid: fast, a little painful, but ultimately freeing.

Don't underestimate the power of deadlines, either. Deadlines are the kryptonite of endless editing. If your project is due at 3 p.m., there's no time for a fourth round of revisions or a philosophical debate about whether "however" is better than "but." Deadlines force you to let go, and sometimes, that's exactly what you need.

Finally, embrace the beauty of imperfection. Some of the most successful ideas and creations weren't flawless. The first iPhone? A little clunky. Early Picasso paintings? Not exactly what he's famous for. What makes your work valuable isn't its perfection—it's that you completed it and put it out into the world. Imperfections add character. Plus, they remind everyone that you're human, not a machine programmed to create spotless spreadsheets.

Learning to let go is about trusting yourself and recognizing that perfect is an illusion. Done is better than perfect, and moving on is better than endlessly circling the drain of "just one more change." Once you've mastered this mindset, it's time to celebrate your completion—and yourself. Let's explore how to reward yourself for finishing without diving back into the endless revision cycle.

Celebrating Completion Over Perfection

Finishing a project is like crossing the finish line of a marathon, except instead of cheering crowds and a medal, you're often greeted with a nagging voice saying, *"But could it be better?"* Perfectionism tries to rob you of that triumphant moment, turning your victory lap into a mental debate about whether you should tweak the font size *just one more time.* It's time to silence that voice and throw yourself a proper celebration—imperfections and all.

Step one: remind yourself that finished is an achievement. You did the thing! You crossed the finish line! Sure, maybe your slide deck isn't Michelangelo-level artistry, but guess what? Michelangelo probably wasn't making PowerPoint presentations. (If he were, do you think he'd have worried about font alignment? Definitely not.) Completion is what counts, not whether your color scheme would win design awards.

Celebrating completion starts with acknowledging the effort you put in, even if the final product isn't perfect. Think of everything that went into the project: the brainstorming sessions, the late-night panics, the snack-fueled focus marathons. Every step you took was a win, and the fact that you saw it through to the end is proof that you've got what it takes. Even if you spent half the time Googling *"how to stay motivated"*—you still made it!

Next, reward yourself like the champion you are. Rewards don't have to be grandiose (though I wouldn't turn down a parade in my honor). A favorite snack, a guilt-free Netflix binge, or simply taking the rest of the day off to bask in your accomplishment can work wonders. The key is to tie a positive experience to the act of finishing, so your brain starts associating *"done"* with *"good times ahead."*

Basically, train yourself like a very smart dog, but with fewer belly rubs (unless you're into that).

Another great way to celebrate is to share your accomplishment with someone who'll cheer you on—whether it's a friend, coworker, or overly enthusiastic family member. Call up that one friend who always says, *"You're amazing!"* no matter what you've done. They'll hype you up and remind you that perfection is overrated. Bonus: saying *"I finished!"* out loud makes it harder for your inner critic to chime in with its *"But is it good enough?"* nonsense.

If you're not into public celebrations, treat yourself to a private victory lap. Blast your favorite song and dance like nobody's watching (because hopefully, nobody is). Or do something totally unrelated to work—take a walk, bake cookies, or dive headfirst into that book you've been meaning to read. The point is to shift your focus away from the project and onto something that makes you happy.

If you're still struggling to let go, remind yourself that every project you complete—flaws and all—is a stepping stone to getting better. Nobody becomes great by aiming for perfection every time; they become great by finishing and moving on to the next thing. So, your presentation isn't perfect? Big deal. The lessons you've learned from finishing it will make your next one even better. It's progress, not perfection, that matters.

To really drive home the celebration, consider making a ritual out of finishing. Maybe it's a silly victory dance, a special treat you only indulge in when a project is done, or even just a moment of quiet reflection where you say, *"Good job, me."* Whatever it is, make it yours. Rituals give weight to the act of finishing and make it feel like a milestone worth celebrating—which it is.

Above all, remember this: the world doesn't need perfect work. It needs finished work. Nobody's waiting around for your project to be flawless—they just need it to exist. By celebrating your completion, you're reminding yourself that you're capable, accomplished, and ready for whatever comes next.

And speaking of what's next, let's dive into how to reward yourself for finishing without falling into the trap of endless nitpicking. After all, the best way to honor a job well done is to keep the momentum going.

Humor About Embracing the "Good Enough" Mindset for Success

The phrase "good enough" often gets a bad rap, conjuring images of laziness or mediocrity. But let's flip the script: what if "good enough" isn't settling—it's liberation? Because let's be honest, chasing perfection is like trying to catch a greased-up pig at a county fair: exhausting, messy, and ultimately unnecessary. Sometimes, "good enough" is exactly what you need to succeed without losing your mind.

Think about it: nobody looks at the Mona Lisa and says, *"Hmm, could've used more detail in the background."* They don't nitpick Shakespeare's plays for being a little wordy or complain that the Leaning Tower of Pisa isn't straight. These works are celebrated, imperfections and all, because they're done. (Okay, the tower wasn't supposed to lean, but let's roll with it.)

Embracing "good enough" starts with recognizing that most people don't notice, let alone care about, the details you're obsessing over. That report you stayed up tweaking until 2 a.m.? Your boss skimmed it in three minutes and only cared about the bottom line. That email you rewrote five times? The recipient read the first two sentences and replied, *"Thanks!"* Stop convincing yourself the world is a panel of hypercritical judges—it's mostly people just trying to get through their own to-do lists.

Here's the beauty of "good enough": it saves you from the spiral of diminishing returns. Spending an extra three hours tweaking something that's already functional doesn't make it 300% better—it just makes you 300% more tired. Those hours could be spent on something more productive, like starting a new project, taking a well-deserved break, or finally organizing your sock drawer.

If letting go feels difficult, try a thought experiment: imagine you're delivering a project for someone else. Would you tell them to spend another two hours polishing something nobody will notice, or would you say, *"This is great—move on to the next thing!"* Odds are, you'd encourage them to wrap it up and celebrate their progress. Now apply that same generosity to yourself. Be your own biggest cheerleader, not your harshest critic.

Another way to embrace "good enough" is to reframe it as efficiency. It's not about cutting corners—it's about allocating your time wisely. If 80% of your effort gets you 100% of the result, why spend another 20% chasing perfection that won't actually make a difference? The 80/20 rule is your new best friend, and it's here to save you from your inner perfectionist.

Let's not forget the joy of imperfection. Sometimes, the quirks and flaws in your work are what make it stand out. That slightly off-center slide? Charming. That typo in your email? Relatable. Imperfections make your work human, and being human is a lot more fun than pretending to be a robot programmed for perfection. Besides, robots don't get snack breaks.

If embracing "good enough" still feels uncomfortable, remind yourself of this: the greatest achievements in life often started with "good enough." That startup didn't launch with a perfect app—it launched with a buggy beta version that people laughed at, then grew into something legendary. Your "good enough" today could be the stepping stone to your greatness tomorrow.

Finally, celebrate the freedom that comes with letting go. When you embrace "good enough," you're giving yourself permission to move on and focus on what really matters. No more fretting over minor details or losing sleep over imaginary flaws. Instead, you can channel that energy into your next big idea—or into the bliss of knowing you've done enough for today.

"Good enough" isn't settling; it's understanding that success isn't about perfection. It's about progress, completion, and the confidence to say, *"This is done, and I'm proud of it."* So go ahead—wrap up that task, high-five yourself, and let's dive into how to reward that awesome, imperfectly perfect effort without letting nitpicking sneak back in.

How to Reward Yourself for Finishing Without Extra Nitpicking

Finishing a project is cause for celebration, but for many of us, that celebration comes with strings attached—like a sudden urge to nitpick the work you just completed. *"I'm done! But wait, should I have used a different font? What if they hate the chart? Maybe I'll just redo the whole thing..."* No. Stop right there. Rewarding yourself means putting down the red pen, stepping away from the keyboard, and letting your project exist as it is: *finished.*

The first step to guilt-free rewards is recognizing that nitpicking is just perfectionism in a fancy hat. It disguises itself as *"improving your work,"* but it's really just fear of letting go. Ask yourself this: will anyone but you notice if you spent another hour tweaking the alignment of the bullet points? Will they even care? (Hint: they won't.) The best reward you can give yourself is freedom from the compulsion to tweak.

Next, declare your work done *out loud*. Say it: *"This is finished."* Write it in bold letters, text it to a friend, or whisper it to your plant

—whatever works. Once you've spoken it into existence, it's harder to go back and start tinkering again. Bonus points if you follow up with a celebratory fist pump or victory dance.

Now, it's time to plan your reward. The key to a good reward is making it something that feels like a treat, not just a standard break. If you normally scroll through social media between tasks, that's not a reward—that's just Tuesday. Instead, choose something special: your favorite dessert, a walk in the sunshine, or an uninterrupted hour with your guilty-pleasure reality show. Make it feel like a prize you've earned, because you have.

If you're worried about unfinished business, set a clear boundary for revisiting your work—*if necessary*. For instance, tell yourself, *"I'll check for major typos tomorrow, but today, I'm done."* This gives your brain permission to relax while also satisfying the part of you that insists there's still something to fix. Spoiler: there probably isn't, but if it helps you sleep at night, schedule that check-in.

Another fun way to reward yourself is by creating a "Finished Work Jar." Every time you complete a project, write it down on a piece of paper and toss it in the jar. Over time, you'll have a tangible reminder of all the things you've accomplished. Feeling unproductive one day? Shake the jar like a magic 8-ball and pull out a reminder of how awesome you've been. Just don't use it as an excuse to start nitpicking old work. The jar is for victories, not revisits.

If you're a goal-oriented person, tie your reward to something meaningful. For example, tell yourself that finishing a certain number of tasks earns you a bigger prize—a fancy dinner, a spa day, or even just that gadget you've been eyeing on Amazon. Suddenly, finishing isn't just about completing the project; it's about working toward something you really want. And no, *"redesigning that report one more time"* does not count as a reward.

For the ultimate reward, do something completely unrelated to work. Go to a movie, try a new recipe, or attempt a puzzle you'll inevitably abandon halfway through. By stepping away from your usual routine, you're signaling to your brain that the task is over and it's time to switch gears. Plus, nothing says *"I'm done!"* like spending the afternoon aggressively Googling *"why cats knead."*

Finally, remember that rewarding yourself doesn't have to be extravagant. Sometimes, the best reward is simply giving yourself permission to relax. Take a nap, stare at the ceiling, or sit quietly with a cup of coffee like a mysterious character in an indie film. The goal is to let yourself enjoy the feeling of being finished without immediately jumping to the next thing—or worse, reopening the file you just closed.

Finishing a project is a big deal, and rewarding yourself is how you celebrate that milestone. Once you've mastered the art of guilt-free rewards, you'll be ready to tackle new challenges with fresh energy and confidence. And speaking of fresh starts, let's talk about how procrastination—when done right—can actually fuel your creativity and set you up for success.

Conclusion

And so, we've reached the end—or at least, the part where we finally stop tinkering and call it "done." If you've made it this far, congratulations! You've embraced the chaotic beauty of procrastination and learned how to wield it as a tool, not a trap. Gone are the days of endless guilt over unfinished to-do lists; instead, you now know how to harness the art of doing *nothing* productively.

Procrastination gets a bad reputation, but the truth is, it's a natural part of the creative process. Some of the best ideas come from those "accidental" breaks—when you're folding laundry instead of drafting your report, or daydreaming about owning a coffee farm instead of finalizing your spreadsheet. By embracing your unique procrastination style, you've turned avoidance into action and distractions into opportunities.

Let's not forget the power of flexibility you've unlocked. Whether it's setting mini-deadlines, reframing pauses as productive, or mastering the art of "good enough," you've proven that you can balance procrastination with progress. You've transformed what used to feel like wasted time into intentional moments that recharge your creativity and focus.

Of course, perfectionism didn't go down without a fight—but you conquered it. By celebrating progress over completion and rewarding yourself for finishing, you've silenced the nagging voice that insists everything must be flawless. Spoiler alert: it doesn't. Life is messy, projects are imperfect, and "done" is always better than "still working on it."

Now, as you step away from this book and back into your beautifully chaotic world, remember this: procrastination isn't your enemy. It's the quirky sidekick on your journey, nudging you to pause, reflect, and occasionally organize your snack drawer. By leaning into its rhythm, you've learned to procrastinate with purpose, balance productivity with rest, and create a life where breaks are part of the process—not a guilty indulgence.

So, go forth, procrastinate wisely, and keep finding joy in the ebb and flow of your unique style of productivity. Whether you're organizing pens, daydreaming about world domination, or quietly sipping coffee while pretending to work, know that you've mastered the art of doing absolutely nothing—efficiently. And isn't that the greatest achievement of all?

A Helping Hand for Fellow Procrastinators

"Procrastination isn't laziness; it's the art of doing everything but the thing you're supposed to do." – Unknown

Hi there, fellow procrastination connoisseur! You've just finished *Procrastination for Overachievers: A Humorous Guide to Doing Absolutely Nothing Efficiently*, where we laughed at our quirks, embraced our chaotic tendencies, and learned how to turn procrastination into our productivity superpower.

Now, I have a small favor to ask...

Would you help someone else embrace their procrastination habits by sharing your thoughts about this book?

Imagine someone just like you—an overachiever, a perfectionist, or a professional daydreamer—stuck in a guilt spiral over everything they "should" be doing. Your review could be the reason they pick up this book, laugh out loud at their own habits, and finally learn how to procrastinate with purpose.

We have one simple mission: to help as many procrastinators as possible turn their quirks into strengths and stop feeling guilty about how they work. Reviews help spread the word and make it easier for others to find this book when they need it most.

Could you leave a quick review on Amazon? It doesn't need to be perfect (we've moved past perfectionism, haven't we?)—just a few words about what made you laugh, feel seen, or rethink how you tackle your to-do list.

Your review could mean one more person realizes that procrastination isn't a failure, one more overachiever learns how to balance breaks and deadlines, and one more reader laughs so hard they cry over their own love of "productive" distractions.

Scan the QR code below to share your thoughts quickly and easily!

Thank you for letting me join you on your procrastination journey. Your time, humor, and support mean the world to me.

Here's to mastering the art of doing absolutely nothing efficiently—and helping others do the same.

With gratitude,

Avery Wells